8939

Becoming a Treasured Teacher
Jody Capehart

VICTOR BOOKS

A DIVISION OF SCRIPTURE PRESS PUBLICATIONS INC.
USA CANADA ENGLAND

Unless otherwise noted, Scripture quotations in this book are from the *New American Standard Bible,* © the Lockman Foundation 1960, 1962, 1963, 1968, 1971, 1972, 1973, 1975, 1977. Quotations marked NIV are taken from the *Holy Bible, New International Version®,* copyright © 1973, 1978, 1984 by International Bible Society. Used by permission of Zondervan Publishing House. All rights reserved. Quotations marked KJV are from the *Authorized (King James) Version.*

Cover Design: Joe DeLeon

Cover Photo/Illustration: Mike Marshall

Interior Illustrations: Terry Sirrell

Library of Congress Cataloging-in-Publication Data

Capehart, Jody.
    Becoming a treasured teacher / by Jody Capehart.
        p.   cm.
    Includes bibliographical references.
    ISBN 0-89693-979-0
    1. Sunday school teachers. 2. Christian education. I. Title.
BV1534.C264 1992
268'.3 — dc20   92-4818
                                                                         CIP

---

        3   4   5   6   7   8   9   10   Printing/Year   96   95   94

Contents

Dedication

This book is dedicated with much appreciation and affection to Dr. Michael Fisher who brought me into the world of church Christian education. I thank Dr. Fisher and everyone at Grace Bible Church for allowing me to serve as the Director of Children's Ministries from 1987 to 1991.

Acknowledgments

I want to thank all the children at Grace Academy and Grace Bible Church for being such a joy to teach and for teaching me so much.

I want to thank my loving brother, Alan Kvanli, and dear friend, Donna Trapp, for their invaluable computer assistance.

I want to thank my parents, Chet and Donna Kvanli, who allowed me to "play" teacher for hours on end and always believed that I was a "born teacher."

I want to thank my younger siblings Joel, Kevin, Kerry, and Lynelle who let me "practice" on them and my older siblings, Bonnie and Alan, who let me learn from their teaching examples.

I want to thank my parents-in-law, Paul and Marjorie Capehart, who introduced me to the world of Dallas Theological Seminary and who have taught me so much.

I want to thank all the wonderful teachers it has been my privilege to teach and serve with over the past twenty years. I have learned so much from you.

Last, but certainly not least, I want to thank my dearest treasures: my husband Paul and our three children, Damon, Christopher, and Angela.

Foreword

This is a hard time to be a child. Every day the media report crimes by and against children. Record numbers of youngsters are neglected, abandoned, and abused. Children hurry into adulthood before they are equipped to meet adult challenges. The suicide rate is rising.

This is also a tough time to be an adult who cares for children. Working parents anguish over placing their children in childcare. Schoolteachers and parents blame each other for the problems and failures of the youngsters they both love. Physicians struggle to help infants with inherited drug dependency or fatal illness. What is to be done?

Author Jody Capehart describes one way to make an important difference in the lives of children. A treasured teacher who instructs by lesson and by lifestyle can guide a youngster into a relationship with his Savior. This special kind of teacher must have the skill to teach effectively, the love to accept a child just as he is, and the spiritual maturity to lead a child to Jesus. This book will be a helpful guide to those teachers who want to develop and devote these qualities to their own ministries.

Let me urge teachers everywhere, the novices and the veterans alike, to sharpen their skills and rededicate themselves to the educational ministry of the church. As childhood continues to erode, so do our opportunities to touch hearts that are still reachable and minds yet teachable. There is an urgent need for teachers who will share God's love with His children.

In the time it has taken you to read this foreword, two infants have been born in poverty. By the time you finish the first chapter, an infant will have died in its first year of life. If you put the book aside without finishing it today, by the time you continue reading tomorrow a child younger than five will have been murdered and 100,000 children will have gone to sleep homeless. If today was a school day, over 135,000 students took a gun to class.

7

Now is the time to gain the skill and knowledge necessary to make the best use of the hours children spend in Sunday School, Bible club, and camp. Now is the time to learn how to build trusting relationships with youngsters. Now may be the only time we have.

Dr. Robert J. Choun
Dallas Theological Seminary

Introduction

Every year in our church we have a Teacher Appreciation Sunday on which we honor the teachers who have taught the adults, youth, and children in our church that year. Two years ago, our Senior pastor, Dr. Michael Fisher said to me, "This year let's honor some of the great teachers of our past as well as present teachers. Please organize a Treasured Teacher Sunday." When I looked at the list of teachers who had taught in our church, it read like the Treasured Teachers Hall of Fame: Chuck Swindoll, Dr. Dwight Pentecost, the late Trevor Mabry. . . .

In the process of interviewing people about whom they regard as a Treasured Teacher, the one who made a significant difference in their lives, a list of common qualities emerged. And the idea for this book sprouted. Within these pages, I will help you understand just what a treasured teacher is.

My primary teaching objective is to create within us a teachable spirit that will help us to be Treasured Teachers. I will share practical information that will help to facilitate that goal. No one teacher will meet all the needs of all her students, but there are certain common denominators that can help us meet more of our students' individual needs.

As I look at my own life, I see that God has carried me through a wide variety of teaching experiences. While sometimes I questioned why it took me so long to get where I was going, I now realize that He used each experience and each child to teach me. I have taught every age and most subjects in public and private schools, secular and Christian schools, and in several states and countries. I have taught the handicapped as well as the gifted. I believe God has brought me full circle to teach me principles of teaching. He has led me to church work and finally, to training teachers around the country. I believe in what I am sharing with you because I have lived it. My endeavor is to make it practical and easy for you to use.

My prayer is that by your testimony and your teaching God will enable you to transform lives for Jesus Christ. There has never been a greater need for trained teachers. What you do is important. You are significant. What you do counts for eternity.

Transformed Teachers

A Treasured Teacher takes time to know herself, and she realizes that much of her teaching style is based upon her learning style.

"Therefore if any man is in Christ, he is a new creature; the old things passed away; behold, new things have come" (II Corinthians 15:17).

The teaching objective of this chapter is to learn to teach like the Master Teacher as we seek to be teachable and strive to understand our spiritual gift and teaching style.

Chapter One

Nature FORMS us,
Sin DEFORMS us,
School INFORMS us,
But only Christ TRANSFORMS us.[1]

Our goal is to be like the Master Teacher, Jesus. When we fix our eyes on Him and seek to model Him in our teaching, a transformation begins.

Teaching Like the Master Teacher

To be a master teacher, we must seek to be Christ-like. In the Gospels we read the words, "Jesus taught" forty-five times. He is referred to as a teacher forty-six times.[2] We can learn so much from Jesus our Master Teacher

● He came from God. As teacher of the Word, we must be reborn into the Kingdom of God.

Jesus answered, "My teaching is not my own. It comes from Him who sent me. If anyone chooses to do God's will, he will find out whether my teaching comes from God or whether I speak on my own" (John 7:16-17, NIV).

● Jesus prayed daily.

One of those days Jesus went out to a mountainside to pray, and spent the night praying to God (Luke 6:12).

● Jesus loved the children and desired that they come to Him. He prayed for and cared for the children. Jesus valued children.

He called a child and had him stand among them. And He said, "I tell you the truth, unless you change and become like little children, you will never enter the kingdom of heaven. Therefore, whoever humbles himself like this child, is the greatest in the kingdom of heaven. And whoever welcomes a little child like this in My name welcomes Me" (Matt. 18:2-5).

● Jesus used a variety of methods. He lectured, led discussions, asked questions, told stories, used life situations to illustrate points, and met one on one with people.

● He was a wise steward of His time. He looked for opportunities to teach and wisely used the teachable moment. His teaching was timely as well as timeless.

● He believed in what He was teaching. He was committed to Scripture and directed His learners by His example. His life modeled what He taught and added authenticity to His teaching.

Seek to Be Teachable

The treasured teacher realizes how important training is to the whole teaching process. The treasured teacher seeks to have a very teachable spirit.

**Anyone who stops learning is old,
Whether at twenty or eighty.[3]
Henry Ford**

The best training comes from modeling. Edward Kuhlman writes in his excellent book *Master Teacher,* "Unlike the situation in schools, where students may seek out a mentor and not find one, Jesus has sought out those He would teach. For those whom He has called, Jesus Christ is THE Mentor, the Master-Teacher above all others. Principally the mentor wants to influence others; he wants to impact lives entrusted to his care. He seeks to form character, mold manners, and leave firm impressions, just as our Lord did with the disciples. Jesus called the twelve disciples to "be with him" (Mark 3:14). Then in close proximity, He nurtured and developed their capacities and enlarged their horizons."[4]

The most effective training you can provide for yourself, in addition to modeling your teaching after Jesus' teaching, is to find a master teacher who will be a mentor for you. Characteristics of such a person include:

born again
loves people, and children in particular
prepared to teach
always ready to learn
grounded in the Word
empowered with prayer
filled with the Spirit

Formal training is also very important. Each of us has ways in which we learn best. Find what works for you and use it. Possibilities include:

● Read books on teaching. Here are some suggestions to get you started.

Education That Is Christian by James E. Plueddemann, Ph.D., Victor Books, 1989.

Teaching to Change Lives by Dr. Howard Hendricks, Multnomah Press and Walk Thru the Bible Ministries, 1987.

Developing the Teacher in You by Wesley R. Willis, Victor Books, 1990.

Master Teacher by Edward Kuhlman, Fleming H. Revell Company, Old Tappan, New Jersey, 1987.

Teaching Young Children by Wesley Haystead, Gospel Light Publications, 1989.

The Master Plan of Teaching by Matt Friedeman, Victor Books, 1990.

• Attend the Teacher Training given by your church. If your church does not have anything like this, urge your Christian Education pastor, or your Sunday School superintendent to provide it.

• Attend Sunday School conventions in your area. These conventions provide a wide variety of seminars at a very low cost. These conventions bring in nationally recognized experts in the field as well as top local people to train and equip workers in the many different aspects of ministry.

• If there is a seminary or Bible college in your town, check into courses for the lay teacher.

• Continue your own personal time in the Word which will help you sink your own personal spiritual roots deeper.

• Allow time in your weekly preparation of the lesson to read the additional sections in your teacher guide. Your teacher's guide contains lots of tried and true teaching tips which will help you develop as a teacher.

• Pray for the Lord to train you as a teacher in His curriculum for you. Whenever I have prayed this, He has provided me with life experiences and people which proved to be invaluable training opportunities.

Understand Your Gifts

I believe each of us has been given strengths and weaknesses. We give our strengths back to God to be used for His honor and glory. We come to Him on bended knees with our weaknesses, and we yield them to Him so that by His sanctifying grace He can be honored in our lives.

When we are born into the Kingdom of God, we are given our spiritual gift by the Holy Spirit. Paul says that spiritual gifts are given to every Christian by the Holy Spirit (1 Cor. 12:7). The purpose of the gift is not to lift up an individual for selfish gain, but to build up the corporate Body of Christ. We are to use our spiritual gift to accomplish the work of the kingdom (vv. 8-9).

In the book *Your Spiritual Gifts,* C. Peter Wagner defines the gift of teaching as "the special ability that God gives to certain members of the Body of Christ to communicate information relevant to the health and ministry of the Body and its members in such a way that others will learn."[5] In the book *Nineteen Gifts of the Spirit,* Dr. Leslie B. Flynn explains, "The gift of teaching is the supernatural ability to explain clearly and apply effectively the truth of the Word of God."[6]

Dr. Flynn goes on to answer the question, "If a person is capable of teaching, will he automatically have the gift of teaching on becoming a Christian?" The answer is, not automatically; only if the Spirit chooses to give this gift.

He continues, "But it is more likely than not that the Spirit will bestow the gift of teaching on one who already has the talent. The Spirit of God, who operates decently and in order, would likely build His gift with supernatural power upon the foundation of the talent already there, but not always.[7] He goes on to differentiate between the *talent* of teaching and the *gift* of teaching.

Both the talent and the gift of teaching have to do with communication of truth. The teacher with the *talent* of teaching can communicate truth and impart knowledge. But it is the teacher with the spiritual gift of teaching who can take the knowledge one step further and help students grow spiritually with the information. The person with the spiritual *gift* of teaching can truly transform lives for Jesus Christ.

How can you tell if you have the spiritual gift of teaching? Consider these questions:

1. Do you enjoy teaching? God intends for us to enjoy serving in His Kingdom. If you are teaching joyfully, you probably have the spiritual gift of teaching.
2. Do you see fruit in your teaching? Is God blessing your teaching ministry?
3. Are others encouraging you in this area?

In reflecting on my life, I see how God has led me. As one of the oldest of seven siblings, I was often babysitting. This led me to babysit outside the home. I played school for hours on end. I helped my teachers in Sunday School and school. My idea of a fun outing was to walk to a school and walk around the outside studying each classroom through the window. God gave me the desire, but because I was not yet a believer, I did not have the gift of teaching. When I became a Christian, the Holy Spirit bestowed the spiritual gift of teaching on me. Teaching is where my heart is.

Look at your own life. To what activities do you spontaneously gravitate. Where is God blessing you? Where do you receive joy and fulfillment? Your answers will help you find your spiritual gift. Go to the Word and read about spiritual gifts in Romans 12, 1 Corinthians 12, and Ephesians 4.

Understand Your Style

Each of us teaches the way we learn best. We will take a closer look at this in chapter 3, but for now let's look at how our learning style affects our teaching.

How You Learn	Your Teaching Tendencies
You learn best when you can see something.	1. Visual aids 2. Books, workbooks, etc. 3. Writing activities
You can learn best in an auditory mode by listening and talking about something.	1. Lecture 2. Question/Answer 3. Dialogue
You learn best when you can touch something.	1. Supply tactile items for students to touch, such as puzzles and games
You learn best when you do something.	1. Dramas 2. Centers
You learn best when the information is of a factual nature.	1. Lecture of factual, objective information

Know the Teacher Types

Teachers come in all shapes and sizes because people are all individuals. There are, however, some observable patterns. As you read these charicatures, exaggerated to make a point, perhaps you will learn a bit more about the type of teacher you are.

Mr. Take Charge

Mr. TAKE CHARGE is the type who likes to take control and so he sees teaching as something to be controlled. He might start out teaching in Junior High because he saw some

16

of the boys goofing off in church: "Those boys need someone to show them who's boss. What they need is some discipline." The TAKE CHARGE teacher wants control.

Through the sanctifying power of the Holy Spirit, Mr. TAKE CHARGE can learn to let God take charge of his teaching and his students.

Mrs. Tenderhearted

Mrs. TENDERHEARTED has blessed children with her love and her compassion. She loves to nurture and guide. Sometimes she just can't bring herself to discipline "those precious little lambs."

It may take her a while, but Mrs. TENDERHEARTED can learn the importance of tough love, the love inherent in good discipline. Then she will be an even better example of God's love.

Mrs. Talkative

It seems as if Mrs. TALKATIVE gets sidetracked by anybody and everybody coming from church to Sunday School. Then she bursts through her classroom door. She is happy to see the children, asks to hear all about their week, and happily shares about her week.

By understanding her teacher type, Mrs. TALKATIVE can begin to let God help her listen carefully to her students.

Mr. Temperate

Mr. TEMPERATE is the peacemaker, the one who blesses us with his easygoing nature. His classroom might sound rather noisy because he can be so easygoing that he doesn't realize the children are getting out of control.

In addition to using his peacemaking skills, God can also show Mr. TEMPERATE how he can discipline the children and still maintain the dignity of his easygoing temperament.

Mr. and Mrs. Thorough and Tenacious

If you want something done well, this is the couple to ask. They are your idealists, your perfectionists; it is their goal to "do it right." They spend hours preparing their lesson every week. You can see them carrying in the visuals, the games, everything they made during the week for the children. They probably left no stone unturned. Mr. and Mrs. THOROUGH AND TENACIOUS, as they are open to God's leading, can learn to become more flexible. Yes, they will still be thorough and tenacious, but they can learn when to let go and let God.

Mr. Technician

This is the teacher who loves to teach with facts and charts. He teaches the children to analyze, to think deeply. He always challenges them by bringing in extra information from commentaries and books that he has been studying. He is most comfortable with objective information. He might say, "You know, there are kids in my class that simply don't want to learn. They're just wanting to talk. But I'm there to teach and I need to teach them as much as I can about the Word of God."

By being open to the Holy Spirit, in time Mr. TENACIOUS can learn to allow the children time to understand things on a subjective level. He might begin to enjoy an occasional discussion.

I hope you can see the beauty of each teacher type. I praise God for His interest in diversity. Each of these teachers has reached some children. Because just as each teacher is different, each child is different. God in His sovereignty created a plan wherein each child would have a teacher to reach him with the Word of God and the plan of salvation. I praise God for these teacher types.

Be Willing to Shift Your Style

There is a term being used frequently these days: *paradigm shift.* The word *paradigm* comes from the Greek word *paradignma,* which is a pattern or map for understanding and explaining certain aspects of reality. Almost every significant breakthrough is the result of someone breaking with traditional ways of thinking. Many inventions came from someone making a paradigm shift in their thinking patterns. Perhaps it is time for us to make a paradigm shift in how we teach.

Most of us teach the way we were taught and the way we learn best, our own learning style. It is difficult for us to break out of our particular pattern because we do it without thinking, but a decision to have a teachable spirit may enable us to make a paradigm shift in our teaching. Perhaps the paradigm shift will occur for us when we begin to build the bridge between what we ARE and what we want to BE.

In this chapter we have looked at types of teachers, and perhaps seen ourselves. With a prayerful attitude, we can begin to look first at how God made us for His purpose and how He has gifted us. We can then add to that what impact our own life experience, training, and learning styles have on our teaching. We can then become what we WANT to be. (Let's be realistic based upon our own personality strengths and weaknesses.) In this process, it may become necessary for us to make a paradigm shift from what WAS to what WILL be.

To illustrate this, let's take an individual who was raised in a very strict, perhaps legalistic school and home environment. By personality, he may be a perfectionist. His training has taught him that learning is a very serious thing and that to be well-educated you must learn in a structured manner. Now let's say that this individual decides to teach three-year-olds. He brings in all his serious ideas and teaches in a most structured manner. The children don't relate, and his teaching does not succeed. By nature, because he is a perfectionist, he will try harder. But, because each of us responds from our own personality and training, he just becomes even more serious and structured. The spiral continues downward as the children relate to him less and less. How does he break the cycle?

Mr. Perfectionist may have to make a paradigm shift in his thinking about what teaching should be. Through having a teachable spirit, he may begin to move away from his serious ways and begin to incorporate methods that are more appropriate for three-year-olds. This very process is not easy for anyone, especially a very serious, structured perfectionist. This change would definitely be considered a major paradigm shift in this thinking. Is it possible? Yes, it is. How? Through a teachable spirit, a person opens to new ideas and methods. Is it easy? No, but by the grace of God, we can do it.

Be a Torch of Light
A treasured teacher is one who lets his light be seen by others. He is willing to be used. He is willing to share the light that he has attained through his own walk with the

Lord. In Luke 8:16, we read "No one lights a lamp and hides it in a jar or puts it under a bed. Instead, he puts it on a stand, so that those who come in can see the light" (NIV).

Part of being a torch of light is giving ourselves the grace to be transparent. This means being open with our students about who we are and what the Lord is doing in our lives. This willingness to be vulnerable can be one of the most effective teaching tools we have. When we are willing to share our mistakes and weaknesses, children listen to us. Why? Because they relate! We can then share how the Lord is working with us and what we are learning, and how our students can benefit. When they see us being transparent with needs, and going to God's Word to discover what God says about this need, and making life-changing RESPONSES, we become a living curriculum from which they can learn. The written Word becomes a living word for our students.

As we are seeking to let our light shine, we must also consider our trustworthiness. Are we trustworthy? Do we keep commitments to ourselves and to others? This aspect of character is one that we should embody as a treasured teacher committed to teaching the Word of God. Let's demonstrate trust in God by surrendering the desires of our flesh to be used for His honor and glory and then, let us seek to be trustworthy in our personal lives as well as our teaching ministry. Our best students may not be those in our classroom, but rather those individuals that we see in our day to day lives who study us to find out what Christianity is all about. Let's be committed to being above reproach.

Treasured Teacher Training

1. What are some of the teaching methods that Jesus, the Master Teacher, employed:

   _____

   _____

2. State goals that you have to enrich your TRAINING as a teacher this year. Consider the following ideas:

   The book I want to read is: _____

   I agree to attend TEACHER TRAINING at my church that will be given _____.

   I want to learn more about _____.

   _____ I will check into the Sunday School Convention in

my area to see what sessions they are offering.
_____ I will take a Bible class.

I will deepen my own spiritual roots by committing to my own personal daily time in the Word. My goal for this year is to _____.

I will observe a Master Teacher this year to learn treasured teacher techniques. The person I want to observe is: _____. I want to learn

_____

I commit to praying daily in order to incorporate the following Treasured Teacher Techniques in my teaching:

_____

3. My spiritual gift(s) is _____
What am I doing to use them to the honor and glory of God? _____

_____

4. Do I have a Teachable Spirit? _____ Do I need to make a PARADIGM SHIFT in my teaching style? _____
If so, what is my plan to achieve this change? _____

_____

5. What is my Teacher Type? _____
How can I best use this in my teaching? _____
What will I need to guard against? _____

Who Will Be My Teacher?

He who knows and knows that he knows,
He is wise, follow him,
He who knows not that he knows,
He is asleep, awaken him.
He who knows not and knows not that he knows not,
He is a fool, shun him.
He who knows not and knows he knows not,
He is a child, teach him.
                    (Author unknown)

Loving Our Learners

A Treasured Teacher takes time to learn how to reach and teach the individual learner and understand the laws of learning.

"Teach me Thy ways, O Lord" (Ps. 27:11).

The teaching objective of this chapter is to understand the individual learner and the laws of the learning process, and thus find more effective ways to reach and teach each individual learner.

Chapter Two

The teacher who makes little or no allowance for individual differences in the classroom is an individual who makes little or no difference in the lives of his students.
William A. Ward

The cone of learning says that we remember 10 percent of what we read, 20 percent of what we hear, 30 percent of what we see, 50 percent of what we see and hear, 75 percent of what we see, hear and talk about, and 90 percent of what we see, hear, talk about, and do. The main message from these statistics is that the more a child can interact with all of his senses, the more apt he is to retain what he has been taught.

Little children are multi-sensory learners. If we observe babies or toddlers, we see them interact with whatever they are doing with all of their senses, often simultaneously. They pick up an item, put it in their mouth, smell it, look at it, and get to really know the item by interacting with it. As a teacher of preschoolers, you will be more successful by allowing children to interact with their senses as part of the learning process.

I have always seen the senses as the key to reaching a child. We must teach to unlock the gates which give us entry to each sensory part of the child. If one gate doesn't open, then we go to the next. The beauty of this is that no gate indicates the levels of intelligence or ability, it is simply a manifestation of our Lord's desire that we each learn as individuals.

I remember a little boy I'll call Johnny. He had been labeled as "not paying attention," and "talking too much." He was also having trouble learning to read. With each passing year, his parents became more frustrated as Johnny's self-esteem crumbled before their eyes. His educational future looked bleak, and he was just seven years old.

When he became my student, I discovered it was true— Johnny did talk a lot, and he could be disruptive. He did have trouble doing his lesson page in his student book.

One day as I stood behind him, I said, "Johnny, follow along with your finger as I read the lesson." I read with a great deal of voice inflection. He followed along and this time, he knew the answers to my questions. I encouraged him to verbalize what he understood of what I had read. He knew it!

This event led us to discover that Johnny learned best when given a chance to HEAR the lesson and then TALK about it. He was also greatly helped anytime he could TOUCH something. Johnny was fine. We just hadn't opened the sensory gates that helped him learn best.

After this experience, my teaching mission became finding those sensory gates within each child and then reaching and teaching each child for our Lord Jesus Christ.

The dictionary tells us that factors in learning include:
- to gain knowledge,
- to become informed,
- to seek understanding,
- to memorize, and
- to find out.

So our goal as teachers of the Word should be helping our students:

- to gain knowledge of the Word,
- to become informed of what God would have us do,
- to seek understanding of God's ways,
- to memorize parts of His Word, and
- to find out what God would have us do in various situations.

So why do we feel that we have often failed in these tasks? Probably we didn't teach our students in the ways that they learn best. Statistics show us that when we teach to the way the learner learns best, learning will take place. How do we find out what that way is? Let's take a closer look at the many items that factor into the learning process.

There are many books on the market that define different learning processes and styles. I have included in this chapter the ones I have found most helpful in working with children of all ages. I want to acknowledge the excellent research done by people in this area including: Dr. Marie Carbo, Dr. Marie Montessori, Dr. Rita and Dr. Kenneth Dunn, Bernice McCarthy, Piaget, Kohlberg, Myers-Briggs, David Kolb, and others.

Each of these people has contributed much to my understanding of the learning process and for each I am deeply grateful. I do realize, however, that most teachers do not have time to do this extensive amount of research; therefore, I have tried to pull together the best principles from each author and put them in a form that can be applied more easily in the church classroom. (If you want to do more research on these individuals and their work, please see the bibliography.)

**If children do not learn the
way we teach them, then we
must teach them the way
that they learn best.**

We Teach the Way We Learn
As we discussed in the last chapter, we all tend to teach the way we learn best. For example, the majority of teachers learn best in the VISUAL mode; therefore, much of the tradi-

tional teaching process is done in the visual mode with charts, visuals, reading, workbooks, etc. Children that are also visual learners respond positively to this teaching because it is in their comfort zone. Since they are being taught the way they learn best in the classroom, this often becomes a very strong factor in achieving a positive self-esteem in the learning process. Often these children may decide to become teachers and when they do, they may teach the same way they were taught and thus the visual track systems of teaching perpetuates itself over the years.

As we take a look at the many components that make up the learning process, let us begin with WHY we are doing this. What is the PURPOSE in understanding our learners?

Purpose

The purpose of understanding our learners better is to reach each child with the message of salvation and to teach the Word of God so that it makes a difference in each student's life. That is our eternal focus as well as the practical application of our teaching. The more we understand HOW to reach each learner, the more effective our teaching becomes.

Plan

Children go through a series of stages in their learning which we call Child Development. Your teacher guide has information in it which helps you understand the age that you are teaching. Take time to read this because it will definitely affect how you teach. Children do not proceed at the same rate up this staircase of child development, but they generally do proceed in the same sequence. An excellent source of information on this would be any book by Dr. Louise Bates Ames from the Gesell Institute.

The following charts are from an excellent teacher training book called *Effective Lesson Planning,* which is also part of a teacher training video series put out by Resources for Ministry, called "High Impact Teaching." (See the book for characteristics of other age-groups.)

Personality

We see life through the grid of our personality. That grid often colors our perceptions of how things are as well as how

2s & 3s CHARACTERISTICS (Preschool)

Physically	Socially	Emotionally	Intellectually	Morally
are extremely active but tire easily	are self-centered	are sometimes timid and easily frightened	have a short attention span	are developing concepts of right and wrong
are developing large muscle control	are dependent on adults	have a strong need to be loved and accepted by adults	have a limited world of experience	are given to external motivation rather than internal motivation
enjoy rhythm activities	are sometimes timid		have a limited vocabulary	
are easily upset by noise and confusion	have a tendency to play alone		are literal thinkers	
			have more difficulty remembering than older children	

2s & 3s CHARACTERISTICS (cont.)

Concepts to Be Grasped	Because 2s & 3s	We
God made my world.	are active but tire easily...	alternate quiet with active activities and plan learning activities in which they can move.
God made me and loves me.	are timid and easily frightened...	give them plenty of pats and hugs.
God sent Jesus.	have a short attention span...	change activities frequently or have many activities from which they can choose.
Jesus loves me and is my special friend.	have a limited vocabulary...	use simple words and only present simple concepts they can understand.
The Bible is a friendly book that tells me about God and Jesus.	are literal thinkers...	are careful to try to teach only concrete concepts and avoid abstract ones.
I can talk to God in prayer.	do not remember as well as older children...	repeat simple concepts throughout the class period, using a variety of methods.
Church is a happy place where I am loved.	are self-centered...	teach them about sharing and showing consideration of others.
I am important.		
I can express love and kindness to others.	are developing large muscle control...	do not expect them to be adept at abilities which require fine motor skills, such as cutting around circles.

we think they should be. Obviously, it is not as simplistic as this, but let's take a look at a few personality types.

Fun Lover

This child measures the validity of a situation by the degree of fun. If he had fun, then he must have learned. These learners are generally your "people people," and they love interacting with others. If you teach in a very serious manner and allow for little interactive time, this learner is probably not having fun. Thus, the child may reject what you have taught him because it simply wasn't fun. Does this mean that we have to bring in a three-ring circus in order to teach Sunday School? No, but it would be wise to do something fun at some point in your hour of teaching.

I remember a teacher I'll call Mr. Huckle. He was so thorough in his preparation and by many standards could be called an excellent teacher. But many children did not enjoy his class. One day one of the students brought in a cartoon book about church life. Why, even Mr. Huckle got a charge out of some of those cartoons. He wisely bought his own copy, made up a transparency each week from one of the cartoons and shared it in his opening. Such a little thing like that transformed the children's responses. They began to look forward to his class just to see which cartoon he had for them.

Perfectionist

These learners are the idealists; they can see the way it "should be," and they want to do it right. They are often more serious than your fun-loving students. They may even get stuck on an issue, whether major or minor because of a temporary "paralysis of analysis." They can see how a project should be done, and then they begin to question their own ability to pull it off. With these learners, we may need to provide a little more encouragement.

These children do not run up and hug you like the fun-loving ones do. In fact, you can't always tell if they like you. They are often so serious. However, it is usually the parents of these children who tell me how much their child looks forward to getting a hug from me. It's true that often the children who need our affection and encouragement the most, show it the least. With a little encouragement, these students often produce the best artwork, in-depth thinking, and pearls of wisdom.

Control Seekers

These learners generally want control at any cost. You can see it in their eyes! They can often be the discipline problems because they want to be in charge and will do anything to win in a battle of wills. We need to give them tasks to be in charge of that we have defined. The words, "You may be in charge of . . ." work wonderfully. We just want to be sure that we have something ready for them to be "in charge of" so they won't try to get control of the entire class. As teachers, we must teach them how to submit to authority. True leadership comes by learning to follow first. This is a very difficult lesson for these children to learn. They truly give us an opportunity to practice our patience.

Peacemakers

These learners are wonderfully easygoing. While the Fun Lover is trying to have "fun," the Perfectionist is trying to be "perfect," the Control Seeker is trying to get "control," the Peacemaker simply "goes with the flow." However, as wonderful as they are to have in class, be aware of two potential liabilities with these students. First, they CAN be stubborn if pushed too hard, especially by a controlling teacher. Also, they are often the ones who make little witty jokes behind your back. When you turn around and glare at the Control Seeker or Fun Lover whom you are SURE said it, the Peacemaker will look innocent. However, he may well be your culprit. The Peacemaker simply has a delightful sense of humor and loves sharing it.

We are each so vitally needed in the body of Christ. We need those who bring love and joy into the body. We need the deep thinkers and creators. We need the leaders. Each learner brings to the classroom something special to contribute. When I look at these strong-willed children and see God calling them into leadership, I become even more committed to guiding them to be godly leaders. But I remember how they exhausted me when I first began to teach. I so wanted to have discipline in my classroom and these children seemed relentless in their desire to control. When I learned how to challenge them to godly leadership, channel that abundant energy through giving them something to be "in charge of," then it became so much easier.

Perceptual Strengths

Each of the sensory gates could also be called a perceptual strength. As we stated earlier, young children learn through all their senses. Somewhere around first to third grade, most children begin to do most of their learning from one sensory gate, or perceptual strength. When we teach to a child's perceptual strength, he is more apt to learn what we are teaching. A wise teacher will vary her methods to provide something for each learner in each lesson. (See chapter 4 for more on this.) Let's take a look at these perceptual strengths:

Visual
These learners do best when they can see something. They respond best with items such as charts, pictures, written words, and maps.

Auditory
These learners do best when they can hear it as well as talk about it.

Tactile
These learners prefer being able to touch in order to learn.

Kinesthetic
These learners learn best when their body is in movement.

This was definitely an eye-opener for me. I wanted all the children in my classroom to sit still and listen to me and then do their page in the student activity book. When they didn't or I had trouble getting them to do it, I would feel angry. When I learned that children learn in different ways (adults also), I prayed for the Lord to stretch me as a teacher and help me modify my teaching to reach these children. As I let some of them talk more, others do more, and I brought in things for some of them to touch, the transformation in my classroom surprised even me. As I watched, the talkers became lawyers and teachers, the touchers became technicians and mechanics, and the doers grew up to be policemen and doctors. I can clearly see why God designed their learning styles in such a special way.

Part of Brain Functioning

Ask yourself, if you have a difficult project to do that requires concentration and some studying, where would you go to do this work? Would you seek out a place that is quiet, contains a desk or table, and contains bright light such as a window or lamp or both?

Or would you go to a place that provides some sound, contains your comfortable chair or your bed, and contains only a dim light or lamp?

The place and conditions you seek out often reflect which part of the brain you are more comfortable functioning out of. For example, learners that learn best in a logical, linear progression and study the parts before they see the patterns would probably seek out the quiet, bright, and structured sitting area. We call this "left brain."

When you seek out a learning environment that has some sound such as music, you like to sit comfortably or even sprawl on the floor or on your bed with only a little light, you may be more of a right brain person. Right brain people generally see the whole picture quickly and then later realize that the picture is made up of component parts. These may be more creative individuals. Yes, you can be both. But under stress or a difficult assignment, we generally go to where we are the most comfortable.

LEFT BRAIN LEARNING PREFERENCES	RIGHT BRAIN LEARNING PREFERENCES
1. Logical, linear progression	1. Sees whole picture
2. Parts to whole	2. Whole to parts
... —— —— —— ——	—— —— —— —— ...
3. Analytic	3. Global
4. Prefers quiet	4. Prefers some sound
5. Prefers bright light	5. Prefers soft light
6. Prefers formal design (Desk or table)	6. Prefers informal design (floor or bed)

PURPOSE:
Know Christ as
personal Savior

**PART OF
BRAIN
FUNCTIONING:**
Left: Parts to whole
Right: Whole to
parts

PLAN:
Child
development

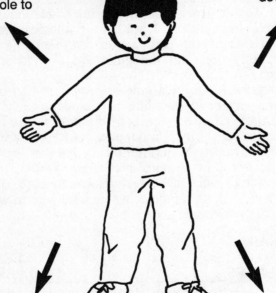

**PERCEPTUAL
STRENGTHS:**
1. Visual: see
2. Auditory: hear, talk
3. Tactual: touch
4. Kinesthetic: move, do

PERSONALITY:
1. Fun Lover
2. Control Seeker
3. Perfectionist
4. Peacemaker

If it is true for us, it is certainly true for our learners. We have all seen those children who rarely sit up straight in their chairs, but sprawl across the chair. They create their own noise if there isn't any present in the learning environment. Perhaps it might be wise for us to give these learners an opportunity to have part of the class time on the floor with some auditory activity such as discussion, music, or drama. In the same regard, we must realize that the left brain child works best when it is quiet and he is seated at a table or desk. (Based on research done by Dr. Rita and Dr. Kenneth Dunn at St. John's University.)

Once again, we always come back to our original purpose: to lead our students to Christ and to teach with an eternal focus. We may have to lay aside some of our prescribed notions that children in Sunday School must sit quietly at a table with a bright overhead light in order to learn best.

Simplifying the Process

In order for us to more effectively reach and teach our learners, let us break these learning patterns down into five types of learners. See chart on page 34.

The Biblical Basis for Loving Our Learners

"These commandments that I give you today are to be upon your hearts. Impress them on your children. *Talk* about them when you sit at home and when you *walk* along the road, when you lie down, and when you get up. *Tie* them as symbols on your hands and bind them on your foreheads. *Write* them on the doorframes of your houses and on your gates. (Deut. 6:6-9, NIV, emphasis mine).

Let's look at this passage in terms of our learners. God wanted the Israelites to internalize His teaching so He presented His word, stated His goal, and then provided for each learner's style. He used a variety of methods to motivate.

Something to see.

"*Tie* them as *symbols* on your hands and *bind* them on your foreheads. *Write* them on the doorframes of your houses and on your gates." (vv. 8-9, emphasis mine).

LOVING OUR LEARNERS

FACT FINDER
1. Learns best when presented facts.
2. Likes programmed instruction, competition, objective lectures, and tests.
3. Prefers to learn facts, black and white objective information.

DOER:
1. Learns best when he is doing.
2. Likes to be actively involved in the learning process and learns best when his body is in motion.
3. Prefers action-oriented learning environment.

TOUCHER:
1. Learns best when he can touch it.
2. Likes manipulatives and "hands on" teaching.
3. Prefers tactual learning.

LOOKER:
1. Learns best visually.
2. Likes visual aids, charts, pictures, and the written word.
3. Prefers quiet learning environment.

TALKER:
1. Learns best auditorally.
2. Likes to listen & to talk and needs both to complete the learning cycle.
3. Prefers sound in the learning environment.

Something to talk about.
"*Talk* about them when you sit at home and when you walk along the road, when you lie down, and when you get up" (v. 7, emphasis mine).

Something to touch.
"*Tie* them as symbols on your hands and bind them on your foreheads" (v. 8, emphasis mine).

Something to do.
Walk . . . Tie . . . Bind . . . Write . . . (vv. 7-9, emphasis mine).

Facts to find.
Our Lord encouraged His people to find and know His commandments.

Treasured Teacher Training
1. We teach the way we _____ best.
2. Define *learning* in your own words:

_____

_____

_____

3. Write or discuss the purpose and importance of each point in terms of understanding the total child:

PURPOSE:

_____

PLAN:

_____

PERSONALITY:

_____

PERCEPTUAL STRENGTH:

_____

PART OF BRAIN FUNCTIONING:

_____

4. Complete the following chart on hemisphericity characteristics and preferences.

LEFT	RIGHT
1. Analytic	1. _____
2. Parts to _____	2. _____ to _____
... __ ___ __ ____	____ ___ ___ ___ ...
3. Prefers _____	3. Prefers some _____
4. Prefers _____ _____	4. Prefers low _____
5. Prefers formal design	5. Prefers _____ design

5. What learning style do you think you are?

_____

6. How does this translate into your teaching style?

_____

How to Put a Lesson Together

> A Treasured Teacher knows the importance of proper planning and commits time to preparing thoroughly.

> *"The plans of the diligent lead surely to advantage, but everyone who is hasty comes surely to poverty" (Proverbs 21:5).*

> The teaching objective of this chapter is to put together an effective teaching lesson in order to teach God's Word in such a way that it becomes a living part of students' lives.

Chapter Three

I wonder how many times I have been asked the question, "How long will it take me to prepare my lesson each week? Time is a precious commodity these days. So, how long DOES it take to prepare a lesson?

In my desire to encourage new teachers, I want to make lesson planning as simple as possible, but I know that it will take a new teacher more time. God grows us into the job.

In this chapter I want to show you how to prepare lessons in the *simplest* way possible. And I also want to show you how to sink your *spiritual roots* deep so your Bible lessons transform your students. If we sow "quick-fix preparation," our lessons may reflect shallow teaching and life application. We live in a society that wants instant everything. But if that is how we prepare to teach God's Word, our work will not bear fruit.

Now let's take a look at what preparing an in-depth Bible lesson entails and then simplify the process into seven steps.

Pray

Prayer is where our teaching should always originate. We will discuss this in more depth in chapter 7. For now we will examine three aspects of our prayer life.

WHY do we pray?
We pray because it is prayer that links us with our Heavenly Father and gives us access to His wisdom and truth. It is through prayer that we receive inspiration and guidance from the Holy Spirit in our teaching.

For WHOM do we pray?
We pray for our students. We pray first for their salvation. Then we pray for them to continue to grow in Jesus, becoming disciples of Christ who hunger to know Him and His Word and who live the Christian life in their world.

WHAT do we pray?
That God would enable us to teach His Word in a.way that transforms the lives of our students. We must pray that with God's help we can urge our students to change and then seek out God's Word to make that change.

It is usually easy to spot those teachers who have bathed their students and teaching in prayer. There is a special bonding that forms between the students in that class as well as an application of the teaching that isn't always present in every class. Oh, how sweet it is to observe teaching blessed by the special anointing that only God can bestow through His Spirit. You feel it when you enter the classroom. How I like to encourage teachers to make prayer the springboard of their teaching.

**You may depend on God;
may He depend on you?**

We must have a prepared life
Teaching God's Word is a process which involves the divine teacher, the Holy Spirit, who seeks to teach through the human teacher. We must ask the Holy Spirit to help us be doers of the Word and not hearers only (James 1:22).

We must view our lesson plan much as a traveler would view a road map, a cook would refer to a recipe, and an architect would rely on a blueprint. It is a guide to help us get to where we want to be. But a careful preparation of material will be useless unless we have carefully prepared our lives.

We must take a good look at ourselves as we evaluate our own personal condition:

- Does my walk match my talk? Is there consistency between what I am teaching my students and what I am attempting to live in my own life?

- Have I confessed the known sins in my life and asked God to reveal to me those of which I am unaware? We all have blind spots. When we ask God to give us a window into our own weaknesses and sins, it can often be painful, but it is so very necessary.

- Am I sinking my spiritual roots deep? The more time I invest in studying the Word, praying and then applying God's truth to my own life, the more effectively I can teach others.

The bottom line is this: AM I GROWING IN MY OWN SPIRITUAL LIFE?

Ponder the Scripture Passage

It is important that we cultivate the habit of teaching from the Word of God and not just from the teacher's guide. As we read and study the passage on our own, we begin to see how the Lord is working in our own lives with this particular Scripture passage. It adds authenticity to our teaching when we can say, "Look what the Lord taught me this week with this passage." Nothing teaches more effectively than authenticity backed up with enthusiasm.

**The mark of an excellent teacher
is not so much the ability
to impart information but
a contagious enthusiasm
for learning.**

As we study the Bible passage eagerly, personally, and thoughtfully, we seek to answer the following questions:
1. Who?
2. What?
3. Where?
4. When?

5. Why?

For example, let's say that we are teaching the passage Proverbs 21:2:

Every way of a man is right in his own eyes: but the Lord pondereth the hearts" (KJV).

All a man's ways seem right to him, but the Lord weighs the heart" (NIV).

Take a minute and write out or think through some of these answers that apply to your lesson:
1. To WHOM is the passage speaking? _____
2. WHAT is the main point of the passage?
   What can I learn from this passage that would make a difference in my life today? _____
   _____

3. WHERE does this verse fall in the context of the chapter? _____
   _____

   WHERE would this passage have practical application to the world of today? _____
   _____

4. WHEN was this passage written? _____
5. WHY was this passage written at this particular time?
   _____

   WHY would it be important for us to consider it today?
   _____

Process the Lesson

We must know the purpose of the lesson

Before I teach any lesson, I ask myself these important questions:
1. What is the TEACHING AIM of this lesson?
2. What student NEEDS do I want to meet?
3. What do I want my students to KNOW at the end of this teaching lesson?
4. What PERSONAL TRANSFORMATION do I want to make in the lives of my students?

If you are teaching from a curriculum, these questions should

GUIDED DISCOVERY LEARNING
bridges the gap between man's view and
God's view of life.

1. Needs, interests, and life issues
are explored as first motivating steps
toward understanding God's Word.

2. The felt needs
show where the
learners are as
they begin the
lesson.

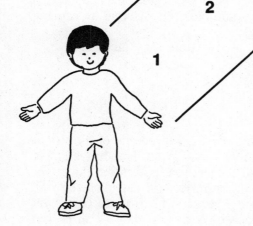

**God's
understanding of
us and our needs**

4

3

2

1

3. Guided Discovery
Learning meets
learners where they
are and guides
them to see life
from God's
viewpoint.

4. These real needs
are the concern of
each lesson.

**Our
experience
and
understanding
of life**

be addressed in your teacher guide. Whether or not they are listed for you, it is still wise to write them out for your own purposes so that you can meet these needs as you prepare your lesson.

It is easy to get caught up in lots of peripheral activities that may detour us from the main avenue and purpose of our teaching. We teach God's Word so that we can build a bridge between the inner needs of our students and the Word of God.

We must provide presession activities

The purpose of the presession activity is to provide something for the students to do as they arrive. This can be related to the lesson or it may simply be focused upon a particular task. The idea is to avoid random behavior that often leads to discipline problems.

Often churches have a break between the Sunday School hour and the church hour, but the children stay in their classroom. The first hour teacher may be cleaning up, and the second hour teacher may want to set up. This can cause a lack of structure to which some children respond by causing discipline problems.

Possible activities to do at this time may include:

- clay
- puzzles
- maps
- centers
- murals

I wish every teacher could have observed one of the teachers I worked with; I'll call him Mr. Carlton. He always got to his classroom early and had at least ten interesting things for the children to do as they entered. He had paper on the wall for drawing, clay for creating, puzzles, pictures to color, felt board lessons for them to do on their own, games that he had made from his old resource packets . . . a haven for the child on the move. The children entered his room with excitement and curiosity wondering what treasures awaited them today. If only we could clone the Mr. Carltons of the world.

We must provide for each learner

If you have a teacher's guide available, it is wise to use it.

Each guide provides:
- professionally prepared material,
- tips for conserving time and work, and
- ideas for teaching more effectively.

However, as you experience the Lord leading in your own life, be open to trying new teaching ideas that He has given you. Again, nothing speaks more clearly than an authentic experience.

Since students process information in different ways, be sure that you have something in your lesson for each learner.

For your LOOKER you can provide:
- pictures
- charts
- graphs
- something to read

In terms of the verse we just looked at (Prov. 21:2), see page 44 for some visuals for your LOOKER.

For your TALKER you can provide:
- discussion
- drama
- dialogue

Remember, while listening is important to the auditory learner, it is the *talking about it* that completes the learning cycle. Be sure that you have given the TALKER time to verbally interact with and about what he is learning.

In terms of teaching the passage from Genesis 4:1-16 in which "Cain has heart trouble," some suggestions may include:

1. Divide the students into two teams. Hand out paper and pencils. As you tell the story, have one team list the characteristics of Cain while the other team lists the characteristics of Abel. After you read the story, they can share their lists. With Cain it may be such things as farmer, no faith, resentful, angry, rebellious, murderer, stubborn, complainer, wanderer, separated from God. Point out that these are heart attitudes. Cain's sinful heart was the cause of his problems.[1]

2. Share personal testimonies of how heart trouble has

43

H E A R T   C HECKUP

Nobody really knows your heart except God. He sees your thoughts and attitudes very clearly. What does he see?

Complete the Heart Checkup Chart. Read each action or attitude. Think about yourself honestly. Circle the number that best describes you.

H E A R T C H E C K U P	Never	Sometimes	Often
Lose my temper easily	0	1	2
Lie to get away with something	0	1	2
Try to get even with those who treat me unfairly	0	1	2
Stay angry a long time	0	1	2
Try to get my own way	0	1	2

TOTAL

Add up your points and write it on the small heart. A total of one or more points means you have heart trouble. None of us is perfect. We all need the Lord to help us be right on the inside and on the outside.

Have you applied God's prescription to your heart trouble? He wants to help you. Don't turn away from Him as Cain did. Have faith in Him as Abel did, and ask Him to be your "heart doctor."

gotten you into a mess. Discuss how sinful acts begin in the heart. Dialogue about why our attitudes are so very important. List attitudes that help us walk our Christian faith and then list attitudes that often get us into trouble.

For your TOUCHER you can provide:
- something to manipulate
- something "hands on"

Most guides will provide an activity in the teacher resource packet. For this passage of Scripture, the Scripture Press Sunday School Curriculum has students mount items on either side of a chart which show behaviors and attitudes like Cain and Abel.

Would not ask God to forgive.

Rebelled against God.

Sinned.

Born with a sin nature.

Asked for God's forgiveness.

Had faith in God.

Sinned.

Born with a sin nature.

@ 1991, Scripture Press Publications, Inc. Used by permission.

For your DOER you can provide:
- drama
- finger plays
- action songs

In terms of this particular lesson, here are some activities you could do.

1. Have two students dress up in Bible costumes and act out the story of Cain and Abel. Tell them to mime the heart attitudes that led to the eventual result. The mimes need to be exaggerated to make the point obvious.

2. Select several children to mime other heart attitudes and see if the other children can guess what they are acting out. Then make a list of what possible sinful acts could occur as a result of each of these attitudes. For example:

Anger $\longrightarrow$ Fighting

Hate $\longrightarrow$ Broken relationships

Refusal to forgive $\longrightarrow$ bitterness, separation

For your FACT FINDER, you can provide:
- Additional Bible background on the Scripture passage from a Bible commentary.
- Additional verses that deal with the lesson.
- A Bible map that shows where the events in the passage occurred.

In terms of this passage of Scripture you could do the following:

1. Have a student identify on a map where Cain killed Abel.

2. Have a student identify on a time line when this event happened.

3. Provide additional verses that depict "heart trouble" and have the student categorize them into classifications of sins such as:

anger
jealousy
refusal to forgive

Point the Way

As teachers, our job is to present information and let children discover and thus internalize what they are learning. The Holy Spirit facilitates the process. The best learning is that which the child, through the aid of the teacher and the Holy Spirit, discovers. Sometimes we think that learning is simply pouring information into the mind of a child, but real learning is a GUIDED DISCOVERY PROCESS.

It begins as we begin to POINT THE WAY toward the lesson's aim by capturing the student's attention and focusing it toward a need that the child may have in real life. The student may not realize that he has this need yet and so part of the process may be raising a question, presenting a possible problem, or creating a scenario in which the child can begin to see himself and thus, his need.

Children often seem to be sure they would be like the Good Samaritan if they saw someone in need. They seem not to see their need to work more diligently to care for their neighbors. They don't see the behavior of the priest or Levite in themselves. I've seen those self-assured "Samaritans" go out and knock each other flat on the playground to get to the slide or swings first, without even seeing the correlation between their behavior and what they had just learned in class. We certainly all have our blind spots. We must help our students see how our lesson is addressing a real need in their lives.

We have to meet students where they live, in terms of their own life experiences. Often children categorize Bible lessons as happening long ago and thus having no relevance to their own situation. It is the job of the teacher to help them see that the sin nature has not changed. It may manifest itself in different ways, but it remains the same. Here are some ways to get the children to focus on the need and thus, the lesson aim.

To facilitate self-awareness, we could ask questions like:

Has something like this ever happened to you?

You got your feelings hurt because you thought your best friend liked someone else better than you. Instead of talking to your friend about it, you just held in your feelings. After a while you realized that you had some anger and hurt in your heart. Then one day your friend said he couldn't play because he had a headache and suddenly you found yourself yelling, "I bet you really don't . . . I bet you really just don't want to play with me." Has something like this ever happened to you?

If that doesn't work, try "HAS SOMETHING LIKE THIS EVER HAPPENED TO A PERSON THAT YOU KNOW?" Once they can articulate the need in general, you can gradually help them to begin to see it in themselves.

Another effective way to encourage self-awareness in your students is to share from your own life experience when you had this need. This can serve as a catalyst to get them thinking and examining their own hearts in light of God's Word.

GUIDED DISCOVERY LEARNING

"They recived the Word with all readiness of mind and searched the Scriptures daily whether those things were so."   **Acts 17:11**

FOCUS: **DISCOVER:**   **RESPOND:**

FOCUS: Capture the students' attention and turn it toward the lesson's aim.

DISCOVER: Help the students discover what the Word of God says and begin thinking of possible implications for their lives.

RESPOND: Guide the students to apply Bible truths to their lives and make obedient responses to the Lord.

Penetrate God's Word

Now comes the exciting part! We get to go to God's Word to DISCOVER what God has to say about our need. WHEN WE HAVE A NEED WE GO TO GOD'S WORD TO SEE WHAT TO DO ABOUT IT. The Bible isn't always written in such a way that children can easily understand it. Also, much of what we learn from the Bible is taught to us through the Holy Spirit working with us in our own lives. Thus the role of the teacher is critically important at this time. We need not only to help them to understand Scripture but also to begin thinking of possible applications of biblical truth in their own lives.

It is my personal opinion that a teacher should:

1. Read Scripture clearly and with great voice inflection.
2. Have the students follow along with their finger.

If your students use several translations, it may be wise to write out the passage for the students and make copies so that they can all follow along with the same translation. Yes, that is more work, but it keeps everyone focused on the same words.

Yes, it is wonderful for students to read aloud, but the main reading of the passage needs to be done in the clearest way possible. If the students each read a verse, they often use different translations, speak at different volumes, and sometimes stumble over the words. The result is that they do not get the benefit of hearing the passage read clearly as a unit with great voice inflection.

I also believe that teachers should teach with their Bibles open. Even if you are using flannels, or your teacher's guide, place them inside your Bible so the students can see that it is God's Word you are teaching from. It is the habit of going to God's Word that we are trying to instill in our students.

I like to write notes in my Bible with a red pencil—must be the teacher in me. One day a playful child said as he looked at my Bible, "Hey, what's black and white and red all over? Mrs. Capehart's Bible!" Then he looked at me for fear that I would be upset at his joke. I only smiled for I want my students to want to look at my Bible and see a book well used and greatly loved. It's like an old friend.

Produce Life-Changing Responses

It has been said that this may be the most difficult part of teaching the Bible because we need to make it applicable to the life experience of our students. It is at this time that we seek to help our students RESPOND to biblical truths and seek to obey the Lord. Our teaching must be consistently biblical, seeking in every phase of the teaching process to link lives to the truths revealed in God's Word. Our teaching must be Christ-centered, leading learners to relate everything in life to Jesus Christ as Lord. Our teaching must be pupil-involved, helping our students of all ages search out God's perspective on issues.

On a practical note, if we want to have our students go to God's Word for dealing with life issues, it would be wise to train them *how* to use their Bibles. It is my conviction that this must be an important part of our curriculum during the primary department years. A few guidelines include:

1. Show them how to divide their Bible in half with their thumbs and then to divide the section on the right once again in order to get close to the New Testament. A few practices with this will enable them to find their way to the New Testament.
2. Teach them the books of the Bible in order. Child Evangelism has a wonderful song and visuals to do this.
3. Give them opportunities to practice looking things up without time pressure. You may even pair the children up, or they can work in groups. Remember there are many adults who cannot find their way around the Bible. Let's be patient with the children as we train them in how to look up passages. The more comfortable and successful we feel in doing something, the more apt we are to do it. Success breeds success. Let's grow children who are comfortable in their Bibles.

Prepare in Practical Aspects

In order to maximize our teaching, we need to be well-grounded in the Word and committed to prayer. Obviously, we need to go through our lesson to know what we are teaching. But there are a few practical aspects that impact our teaching as well.

1. PRACTICE teaching your lesson so you will be comfortable with the information
This doesn't mean going through every aspect with a live audience, but it does mean going over the material a few times. Lookers process best when they write out what they are going to do. Talkers often need to discuss it. Doers need to DO something to internalize the lesson. Find out what you are and work with your strength as you prepare to teach. The more comfortable you are with what you teach, the more likely you are to have a positive teaching experience.

2. PURCHASE the items you will need that your curriculum or church cannot provide
Each church has its own policy on this. Some have you turn in your orders to the person in charge, and he makes the purchases. Some churches have you purchase your own supplies and then you are reimbursed. Others say that whatever you purchase needs to come out of your own pocket because of the church's limited resources. If your church cannot provide materials, it may be wise to consider purchasing one item a month and keeping them in a handy carrier to bring with you each Sunday. For example: glue, crayons, scissors, tape, markers, and clay.

3. PROVIDE enrichment activities
Look at the end of the teaching section for ideas on how to enrich the teaching lesson. Often this section is full of ideas for our individual learners. If not, you may simply want to get into the habit of adding some of your own ideas. Make up a form similar to the following, or you may photocopy the page.

For the LOOKER I will also provide: _____

_____

For the TALKER I will also provide: _____

_____

For the TOUCHER I will also provide: _____

_____

For the DOER I will also provide: _____

_____

For the FACT FINDER I will also provide: _____

_____

Teaching to Changes Lives for Jesus Christ

As you teach, pray to have an eternal focus. Let's not just think of teaching as something to check off our "To Do List" for the week. Pray that the Lord will use your teaching to make a change in a child for eternity. The most significant thing you can do for a family is lead their child to Christ. Practice the presence of God in your own life so that you feel filled with His Spirit as you enter your classroom to teach. Pray for God to give you a practical application in your own life with the lesson so that you can share that with children in your teaching. Pray to teach to change lives and by God's grace, you will!

> Dear Lord, I do not ask
> That Thou should'st give me some
> high work of Thine.
> Some noble calling, or some wondrous task.
> Give me a little hand to hold in mine;
> Give me a little child to point the way
> Over the strange, sweet path that leads
> to Thee;
> Give me a little voice to teach to pray;
> Give me two shining eyes Thy face to
> see.
> The only crown I ask, dear Lord, to wear
> Is this:
> that I may teach a little child.
> I do not ask that I may ever stand
> Among the wise, the worthy, or the
> great;
> I only ask that softly, hand in hand,
> A child and I may enter at the gate.
>   Author Unknown

Treasured Teacher Training

1. I've included a planning guide to help you plan your lesson on pages 55 and 56. You may photocopy this on an 8½ x 11 piece of paper and use it as one horizontal sheet OR fold it in the middle and place in it your Bible. Make this work for you as a help and not a hindrance. For example, if you are a LOOKER, you may want to write out the answers and fold the sheet in the middle, place it in your Bible, and teach from it. If you are a TALKER, you may only want to talk it through with yourself or someone else. If you are a DOER, you may want to actually do part of the lesson. Remember, this may help. Make it user friendly.

2. After you teach a while, you may only need a checklist to help you plan your lesson. Perhaps the outline below may be of help to you. If so, make copies and simply place this in your Bible.

_____ **Pray:** Have I prayed about my
_____ students?
_____ lesson?
_____ teaching?
How does my spiritual barometer read?

_____ **Ponder the Scripture passage**
_____ **Process the lesson:**
_____ What's the PURPOSE?
_____ What PRESESSION activity do I have?
_____ How will I bring my students to discover what God says in the passage?
_____ **Point the way:**
_____ Have I helped my students see their need for what I am teaching?
_____ **Penetrate God's Word:**
_____ Have I PROVIDED something for each learner?
___ LOOKER
___ TALKER
___ DOER
___ TOUCHER
___ FACT FINDER

_____ **Produce Life-Changing Responses:**
_____ How can I encourage life-changing responses in my students?
_____ **Prepare Practical Aspects:**
_____ Do I have appropriate supplies?

3. After a while, each step will become second nature to you. Then you will automatically prepare with this outline in your mind.

_____ **Pray**
_____ **Ponder the Scripture Passage**
_____ **Process the Lesson**
_____ **Point the Way (Focus)**
_____ **Penetrate God's Word (Discover)**
_____ **Produce Life-changing Responses (Respond)**
_____ **Prepare in Practical Aspects**

4. Select the form with which you feel most comfortable and plan your next lesson. God's Word does not return void. Prepare and watch how the Lord will use His Word in your life to help others. God bless you in your planning and preparation.

PLANNING MY LESSON

Lesson _____

Date _____

Unit Theme _____

Scripture _____

Bible Truth Aim _____

_____

Life Response Aim _____

_____

Memory Verse _____

_____

Plan for Teaching Verse _____

_____

_____ Prayer Daily

_____ Ponder Passage Daily

_____ Provide Materials

_____ Prayer Requests

_____ Presession Activity _____

_____

_____ Provide Enrichment _____

_____

_____ Prepare Resources _____

_____

Point the Way   FOCUS

_____

_____

Passage   DISCOVER

_____

_____

Present for each learner

    Looker _____

    Talker _____

    Doer _____

    Fact Finder _____

    Toucher _____

Produce Personal RESPONSE (application)

_____

Present Plan of Salvation _____

_____

Pupil's Book _____

Projects _____

Participation in Centers _____

Provide Worship _____

_____

Personalize _____

Powerful Praying

A Treasured Teacher trusts in the power of prayer and regards praying for her students as a God-given privilege.

"Be anxious for nothing, but in everything by prayer and supplication with thanksgiving let your requests be made known to God" (Philippians 4:6).

The teaching objective of this chapter is to effectively pray for our students because we understand the purpose and power of prayer in our own lives.

Chapter Four

"Prayer is the central avenue that God uses to transform us."[1] Real prayer is life-creating and life-changing. William Carey writes, "Prayer, secret, fervent, believing prayer lies at the root of all personal godliness."[2] All who have walked with God have experienced prayer as the main business of their lives. Martin Luther said, "I have so much business I cannot get on without spending three hours daily in prayer."[3]

We all understand prayer is important and sense the need to pray more for our students. So, what prevents us from practicing that which we know to be true?"

Prayer is a battle each of us faces. In his autobiography, a prayer warrior whom I admire very much said that every morning he underwent a battle before he finally got up and got praying. It is a battle. When we realize this we can learn how to win in the battle.

Our students learn far more from WHO we ARE than from what we say. Who we are is determined largely by our commitment to prayer. This chapter gives us practical tools to win in this important battle.

In my conversation with Mrs. Smith, she told me how she had learned to pray for her students.

"Praise God there have been great prayer warriors over the years to be our examples. God used the lives of others to teach me how important prayer is in our teaching ministry. After I had been teaching for seven years, the Director of Christian Education asked if I would be the Primary Department Head. I accepted that responsibility, although I felt inadequate in many respects. It was I who learned from this experience.

"One teacher in the Primary Department came early every Sunday morning. She went into her classroom and quietly prayed. One day, as I delivered the 'Take Home Lessons,' I saw her praying through a set of notecards. It aroused my curiosity. She said she kept a card for each student in which she wrote prayer requests, and this helped her to pray specifically for her students each week. The difference in her class was obvious. Children seemed to blossom the year she was their teacher. What a testimony to prayer this woman was!

"I began to do the same for my own class. I arrived five minutes early to 'bathe the room in prayer.' I began to notice a difference. After a few weeks, I wrote a notecard for a student that I knew was going through a divorce at home. God showed me a way that I could reach out to this child. A month later I wrote another card for a child that frankly had been getting on my nerves. Again, God gave me insight to understand this child's feelings and showed me what I could do to reach him. By Christmas he gave his life to the Lord. In fact, he is now an effective leader in our church and has a teaching ministry for troubled boys. God was leading me in this exciting journey called PRAYER.

"The following year I had my prayer-warrior friend share with the other Primary Department teachers how she prayed for her students. I shared what I had learned from her and put into practice as well in the past year. Our department became a POWERHOUSE OF PRAYER. The impact began to ripple out to our church and led to a PRAYER REVIVAL that transformed our church. There is power in prayer. The key is simply to begin with that first step. God will do the rest. Praying for that student who may annoy you will allow the Lord an opportunity to bond the two of you in Christian love."

**When we depend on people, we
see what people will do. When we
pray and depend on God, we see
what God will do.**[4]

Personal Experience in Prayer

On a personal level, I have found that during times of major crises I have experienced the most peace. I attribute this to the power of prayer. I have learned from painful experience not to leave for a speaking trip unless I know that several people are praying for me. Without their prayer, I find that my luggage gets lost, or my slides fall out, or I may get sick. I know when others pray for me by a special presence that cannot be explained apart from prayer.

After I resigned as principal of a school for fifteen years, the school went through two principals during a difficult transition time. Some families and teachers began to leave the school. Then a person deeply committed to prayer was hired. It was evident that she bathed every aspect of the school in prayer, and a beautiful transformation began to occur. People returned, and peace and order permeated the school. What a testimony to the power of prayer!

Prayer Modeled by the Master

In John 17 we see how the Lord prayed:

1. Himself
2. His disciples
3. All believers

Jesus gave us a model prayer in Matthew 6:9-13. He told us where to pray (Matt. 6:6). He also said "If you abide in Me, and My words abide in you, ask whatever you wish, and it shall be done for you" (John 15:7).

Passages to Ponder

The Bible says much about prayer. Take time to look up some of the following passages and select one that specifically ministers to you. Commit it to memory. Pray about it. Ponder it as you go about your daily activities. See what God will teach you through these verses.

> Ask, and it shall be given to you; seek, and you shall find; knock, and it shall be opened to you. For everyone who asks receives, he who seeks finds, and to him who knocks it shall be opened (Matt. 7:7-8).
> And this is the confidence which we have before Him, that if we ask anything according to His will, He hears us. And if we know that He hears us in whatever we ask, we know that we have the requests which we have asked from Him (1 John 5:14-15).
> Then you will call upon Me and come and pray to Me, and I will listen to you (Jer. 29:12).
> If you shall ask the Father for anything, He will give it to you in My name. Until now you have asked for nothing in My name; ask and you will receive, that your joy may be made full (John 16:23-24).
> And whatever you ask in My name, that will I do, that the Father may be glorified in the Son. If you ask Me anything in My name, I will do it (John 14:13-14).
> But you, when you pray, go into your inner room, and when you have shut your door, pray to your Father who is in secret, and your Father who sees in secret will repay you (Matt. 6:6).

You will be blessed by finding more Scriptures on prayer.

Roadblocks to Prayer

As Paul said in Romans 7:15, "For that which I am doing, I do not understand; for I am not practicing what I would like to do, but I am doing the very thing I hate." These are words to which most of us can relate. We want an effective prayer ministry for our students. What prevents us from being more effective? Let's look at some of the roadblocks that keep us from developing a fruitful prayer ministry.

Satan

We are commanded to "Put on the full armor of God, that you may be able to stand firm against the schemes of the devil.

For our struggle is not against flesh and blood, but against the rulers, against the powers, against the world forces of this darkness, against the spiritual forces of wickedness in the heavenly places" (Eph. 6:11-12). Even Jesus had to get Satan to leave Him alone. How did He do it? He quoted Scripture to him. We need to have a verse to say out loud the next time we feel Satan trying to stop us from having a powerful prayer ministry.

Sin
We may have unconfessed sin in our lives that is preventing us from having an effective prayer life. We need to ask the Holy Spirit to reveal sin to us that we are unaware of. "If we confess our sins, He is faithful and righteous to forgive us our sins and to cleanse us from all unrighteousness" (1 John 1:9).

Selfishness
Selfish purpose robs us of the power of prayer. We need to SEARCH ourselves. What is our motive in praying for something? "If I regard wickedness in my heart, the Lord will not hear" (Ps. 66:18).

Low self-esteem
Sometimes we think God will never answer our prayers because we are too unworthy. God does call us to have humble spirits, but He also wants us to come to him as little children, believing. Rom. 8:26 tells us, "And in the same way the Spirit also helps our weakness; for we do not know how to pray as we should, but the Spirit Himself intercedes for us with groanings too deep for words."

Spirit
A spirit of unforgiveness may keep us from receiving the blessing of forgiveness ourselves. "And whenever you stand praying, forgive, if you have anything against anyone; so that your Father also who is in heaven may forgive you your transgression" (Mark 11:25).

Practical Steps to Prayer
Just as there are roadblocks that keep us from a more effective prayer life, there are steps that can help us attain a more

powerful prayer life. Let us use the following steps to counteract the roadblocks that Satan would put in our way.

Prioritize

Make prayer a priority. There is wisdom in putting prayer first in our day because we all know "later" never comes. Life can fill our days and consume precious moments we could have spent with our Lord. There are some familiar adages that sum this up so well:

**One week without prayer
makes one weak.**

Life is fragile, handle with prayer.

Purify motives

A PURE heart before God can enhance our prayer ministry.

Praise

When we feel empty, if we simply begin to praise God for all He has done for us, we can experience His presence. Reading Psalms is a good way to start us down the road to praise.

Prepare to seek the face of God

Persist even when we don't feel like it

Pray God's promises from His Word

Pray

Ask God for a Christlike character rather than just a temporal answer to a need. Circumstances change, but character is developed.

Trust in His provision

Pray in the power of His Spirit

Pray believing

Petition

Pray in the name of Jesus

- **Steps *to* an effective prayer life**
- **Roadblocks to an effective prayer life**

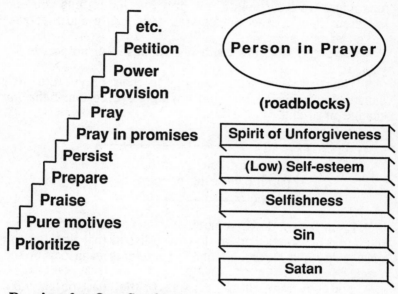

Praying for Our Students

What a privilege it is to pray for our students. Charles Stanley writes, "Our prayers are the link between God's inexhaustible resources and people's needs."[5] However, we may not always know the needs of our students.

A way that helps me pray for my students is to always have some 3 × 5 notecards with me or in a box in the classroom. I give the students some time during the hour in which they can write down their prayer requests. These are often different than the requests shared during our class prayer time. I keep these private. As the year progresses, the children open up more. My praying for their requests strengthens the bond between us as well. It is as if the Lord builds bridges between our souls through this time of prayer. I can look in their eyes on Sunday, or they share something as if to let me know they know that I am praying for them. We share the joy of answered prayers. We grow as we learn that sometimes God answers "no." All in all, it deepens our spiritual journey together.

There are different ways to begin to pray for your students. First, you obviously have to be committed to doing it. Second, find a system that works for you. Perhaps the following idea might work for you. If not, pray for God to help you find a system that is practical for your personality and lifestyle.

To get you started:

● Have the students write out requests on notecards for you.

● You write out notes relating to their prayer time requests. Perhaps you may be praying for a certain behavior change in a child. For example:

> I pray for Johnny to be more patient with his peers.

● Simply pray down your class roster. You could pray for one child per week and go down the list in that way, or you may pray for a certain number of students each day of the week.

● You may want to make copies of the chart on page 65. Put the name of each child in the center of a page. Pray through each of the areas on the chart or simply highlight areas of special concern that you have for each child. Don't get overburdened trying to pray in all categories for each child every day. You don't have time and will get discouraged. Remember, the purpose is to build an effective intercessory prayer life for your students, not to create more work for you. View prayer as a ministry, and the Lord will help you to carry the load.

Praying with Our Students

The most effective way to teach prayer is to model prayer. In January 1991, people were just arriving for Wednesday night church activities when war in the Mideast was declared. In

Praying for Your Students

Child's name

1. Personal relationship with Christ
2. Put Jesus first
3. Powered by the Holy Spirit
4. Praising God in word and deed
5. Prayer warrior
6. Purpose to love and live in the Word
7. Participate in worship

Continue on in concentric circles:
8. Protection
9. Peer relationships & role models
10. Provision
11. Practical application
12. Promote evangelism

each classroom, we read to the children from Ephesians 6, and then we prayed together. Prayer was a big security blanket that we wrapped around each child. In times of stress and confusion, prayer models for our students what to do—we go to our Heavenly Father and talk to Him.

Prayer should be a part of each hour in our church programs. Again, children learn more from our attitudes about prayer than from what we say about prayer. If we are excited to pray, it will be contagious to our students. If we are consistent in prayer time, we will train our students in the habit of prayer.

Practical Prayer Projects

Several ways to train students in prayer habits are found in chapter 7 of my book, *Cherishing and Challenging Your Children*. Let's take a look at two of these.

For preschoolers

We fold our hands. As we wiggle our thumbs, we say, "Prayer is talking to Jesus. What do you want to tell JESUS? We can thank Him, praise Him or tell Him something.

"Our next three fingers remind us to pray for others. Who do we want to pray for? Our family? Our friends? Our missionaries? Our teachers? Those who are sick? Those in our church? Let's pray for OTHERS.

"As we wiggle our little finger, we think of ourselves. What do you want to pray for? What do you want to tell Jesus that you need?"

This process trains preschoolers to put Jesus first, others next and "you" last. The three letters, of course, spell JOY.

For elementary age children

You can train older children in principles of prayer such as praise, confession, thanksgiving, and supplication. Be sure that you take time to talk about what each means before teaching this prayer technique. (See Appendix A for other prayer projects.)

Since prayer is a privilege, I tell students the reason we close our eyes and fold our hands for prayer is to focus our complete attention on God. If we're looking around or fidgeting with something, we are less likely to be focused on the

Lord. Does God answer prayers of only the children who sit quietly and close their eyes and fold their hands? No. God answers the prayers we pray from our hearts, but quiet hands help our hearts to be more quiet.

Prayer partners
Children come to an age when they may not be comfortable sharing personal prayer requests with the entire class. This may be the time to introduce the idea of prayer partners. Pair each student with a classmate that you feel will be a compatible prayer partner. Allow time each Sunday for them to pray together. Stress that this is a time of prayer and not gossip or play. It is very important to train our students in the wisdom of not repeating a person's prayer requests as gossip. Nothing will hurt students more and compromise their ability to be vulnerable. For example, a student may carry a burden for a long time because he has a parent who drinks. In disclosing this personal secret and the pain of the situation, he is blessed to know that people are praying. However, if word that "so and so's father drinks" reaches the child's parent, he will be furious. A vulnerability shared in an atmosphere of trust now becomes a liability. How sad. How unnecessary. Please, let's respect each other's right to privacy.

The best way to strengthen a muscle is to use it. Exercise your prayer muscle today.

A Teacher's Prayer

I want to teach my students how
To live this life on earth —
To face its struggles and its strife
And how to improve their worth —
Not just the lesson in a book
On how the river flows —
But how to choose the proper path
Wherever they may go —

Becoming a Treasured Teacher

> To understand eternal truth
> And know the right from wrong —
> And gather all the beauty of
> A flower and a song —
> For if I help the world to grow
> In Wisdom and in grace —
> Then I shall feel that I have won
> And I have filled my place —
> And so I ask your guidance, God
> That I may do my part —
> For character and confidence
> And happiness of heart.[6]

Treasured Teacher Training

1. Examine your own attitude about prayer. What do you believe about the power of prayer in terms of your own life experience?

   _____

   _____

   _____

   _____

2. Write a Scripture passage on prayer that really ministers to you.

   _____

   _____

   _____

3. List some of the roadblocks that may have hindered you from having a more effective prayer life.

   a. _____

   b. _____

   c. _____

4. List steps to help you to a more effective prayer life.

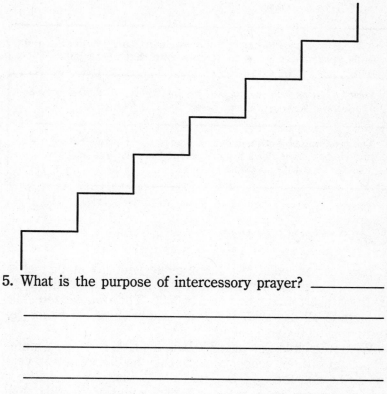

5. What is the purpose of intercessory prayer? _____

_____

_____

_____

6. Select a way to begin praying for one of your students this week. Pray for this student for one month. Share the results here or with someone.

_____

_____

_____

_____

_____

Need for Nurturing

A Treasured Teacher sees the need for nurturing students and finds appropriate ways to demonstrate that nurturing.

"Beloved, let us love one another, for love is from God; and everyone who loves is born of God and knows God" (1 John 4:7).

The teaching objective of this chapter is to remind us that we need to find appropriate ways to nurture our students; this includes embracing those with special needs.

Chapter Five

A two-year-old child was home alone with his mother after his father left for work around 8:00 in the morning. His mother had a heart attack and died at 8:30. The traumatized child was alone all day with his dead mother until his father returned at 6:00 that evening.

When the child was in grade two, his father and new mother sought out our school because they had heard it was very nurturing and loving. They felt it was what he needed in a school experience in order to heal. I agonized for this child and realized the situation would be difficult. We prayed about it; I felt the Lord saying "yes," and we took the child.

He was a major challenge. Sometimes for no apparent reason he would begin to scream or cry. Many days I carried him down the hall as he screamed, and I rocked him for hours in my office. The classroom teacher met with him each day before class and prayed with him. She was a tremendous nurturer and did much to facilitate the healing in this child. One day after chapel, I found him sobbing in a fetal position. I stayed with him as he cried, "I feel love ... I feel love ... I feel Jesus loving me ... " and he accepted Christ that day. Yes, love does heal.

I strongly believe that children need to be touched and

nurtured. Without love, our teaching remains on the pedagogical periphery, and does not impact or mold our students internally where true teaching takes place. Our words remain hollow if we do not bond them to our students with our love.

There is a great need for nurturing today. Children often come to us from very difficult home situations. Statistics tell us that 50 percent of our children come from broken homes and that an even higher percentage come from dysfunctional families. Children are often hurting, bewildered, and angry.

As Treasured Teachers, we can be as an oasis of love for them. They can cling to us in the raging storms of life, and we can bring them to the stability and peace Jesus Christ offers. We can do much to keep them from going adrift in a world that often doesn't care. The need for nurturing teachers that truly love their students abounds.

As a principal, I looked carefully for the degree of nurturing in a teacher. I preferred to have a loving, nurturing teacher with one degree in teaching than a highly trained, multidegreed teacher who could not nurture children. We experienced the fruit of this decision as parents came to observe our school. Their consistent feedback was, "This is a very loving school."

I am a self-proclaimed "rocking chair therapist." To me a rocking chair exemplifies nurturing. In a classroom it is a neon sign that flashes, "I love my students."

Before I had my own children, I observed the trend of the seventies for more mothers to work outside the home. I was concerned about the lack of nurturing these children would experience. I designed a "model day-care center" with a room in the middle that was the nurturing center. It had wide, open, bright areas, a cozy corner with pillows, lots of baskets of books, and rocking chairs everywhere. This was the "Rocking Womb." I wanted moms to come here anytime during any day and nurse, nurture, and be with their children. I designed a lunchroom for moms or dads to eat with their children. At the time I felt tremendously excited because I saw the center as a "win-win" for children and their parents. I was contacted by several corporations and given well-padded budgets to develop nurturing centers for their employees.

Something was wrong, however. Finally I realized that if I

71

provided this warm, loving, nurturing environment, I would make it too easy for some mothers to work outside the home. I wrestled for a long time with this. My heart ached for the children whose moms *had* to work. I wanted to nurture them with everything I had. In fact, I often invited kids to come home with me to spend the night. I knew how much they needed that extra bit of nurturing. Just as a flower opens up when given proper sun, water, and soil, so does a child when given attention, a gentle touch, encouragement, and a nurturing environment.

After much soul-searching, I did not provide these centers, and I began to pray for more moms to find ways to be home with their children. I began to encourage nurturing friends to open up home child care for moms who *had* to work.

Appropriate Nurturing

We must be sensitive about how we nurture. What is appropriate touch? I believe little children should be held, hugged, and rocked. In the elementary years, a hug remains appropriate for many children. As they begin to develop physically, a sideways hug becomes more appropriate. As children become self-conscious about hugs, I find that just a pat as I pass their desk or chair is enough. As a child becomes self-conscious about outwardly expressing his care, he finds more subtle ways to touch: standing especially close as he asks a question. Since I'm a toucher, I let children sit or stand close. I still hug, pat, touch, and squeeze a shoulder. I often hear parents tell me that their child seeks me out to get "their hug." My personal belief is that we all need love; we just become more sophisticated in how we express love. If a child can receive enough positive and appropriate nurturing, he won't be as vulnerable to inappropriate physical outlets.

Being a visual person, I love pictures. One of my favorites is Jesus cupping the face of a child and tenderly looking into the child's eyes. The other children are close by and His touch is so evident. I believe in my heart that is how Jesus would be around children. I believe teachers need to nurture their students with a tender, yet tough, love. John, the apostle of love, writes in John 13:1, "Having loved His own who were in the world, He loved them to the end."

Dr. Howard Hendricks says in his "Following the Master

Teacher" from the *Christian Educator's Handbook on Teaching,* "Jesus was the quintessential Teacher. He provides the teaching template, the paragon of pedagogy. He was the ultimate authority and prototype for teaching though He never discussed the subjects. His actions modeled the discipline."[1]

Lois LeBar succinctly states, "Christ Jesus was the Master Teacher par excellence because He himself perfectly embodied the truth. He perfectly understood His pupils and He used perfect methods in order to change people. He Himself was 'the Way, the truth and the life' (John 14:6). He knew all men individually and He knew human nature, what was in man generically."[2]

There are different levels of nurturing and Jesus responded to each. *Physically,* He touched people. He held children. He healed. *Emotionally,* he encouraged and nurtured. Jesus, of course, had no hidden agendas or co-dependent motives. He loved children. *Mentally,* He used simple examples from their own life experiences to teach profound, life-changing lessons. *Spiritually,* He was the **living** Lamb of God. He showed men the Way, the Truth, and the Life. **He was the Good Shepherd.** We can learn so much from His example.

Each of us knows ways to nurture with which we are comfortable or uncomfortable. Find the ways that work for you. Here are some suggestions:

Physically
- Eye contact
- Being close
- Hugs
- Pats on the shoulder
- Rocking

Emotionally
- Praise
- Affirmation
- Encouragement
- Giving extra time

Mentally
- Sharing something you've researched because it interests a student.

- Reading a book of special interest.
- Nurturing and encouraging a child's best *efforts*. Look at the *process* instead of the end *product*.

Spiritually
- Sharing God's love with students by *actions* first.
- Sharing the Good News of God's love for us.
- Living the Gospel by your life of loving your students.

> You are writing a gospel
>   a chapter each day
> By deeds you do
> By words that you say
> Men read what you write
> Whether faithless or true.
> Say, what is the gospel
>   according to you?[3]

Why Nurturing Is a Part of the Teaching Process

Why is nurturing important in the process of teaching in the church? Dr. James E. Plueddemann writes in *Education That Is Christian:*

> The focus in teaching is for the pupil to hear God speak a personal word to him and for him to respond personally. The Lord always takes the initiative, in love revealing Himself and His will. We teachers work with Him to get the pupil ready to listen in the context of his or her daily life, which is the only situation that has meaning for him or her. Revelation demands response. God says, "I have made all this provision for you; I expect this of you in return." He wants to set up personal relationships with each pupil, ever more intimate. Christianity is person-to-person.[4]

Some ABCs of Nurturing

We will look at some practical ways to express nurturing both in and outside of the classroom.

A—Accept our learners as God made them.
    Affirm our learners.

When we affirm someone, we are saying that he has value. This does not mean that we approve deeds that are wrong. It means that we are loving the sinner but not the sin.

Affirming statements that enhance self-worth may be:
- "You added much to our discussion in class today."
- "I appreciate having you in my class."
- "You have such interesting ideas."
- "You made an excellent observation."
- "Your loving ways add much to our classroom."

B—Believe in your students.
Many children have no one that simply believes in them. Church could be the only place that children find someone who truly believes in them.

C—Celebrate their birthdays.
There are many ways to celebrate birthdays. The very fact that you know and acknowledge birthdays is a celebration in itself. Tangible ways to celebrate include the following ideas.

Preschool:
Bring a cake, light candles, and sing "Happy Birthday." You may want to add a new verse that says:

"God is blessing you now.
God is blessing you now.
God is blessing you, (Donna).
God is blessing you now."

Primary:
You may bring in a special snack. However, this is a great age to introduce the idea of how old a child is in Jesus. Whenever someone has a birthday, you can use it as a time to share the Gospel. If the child has accepted Christ, you can ask him to share his testimony. Then the other children can figure out how old the child is in Jesus and sing two birthday songs; one for his earthly birthday and the second for his spiritual birthday. This provides a wonderful opportunity for children to share their testimonies. It also helps them to remember and articulate WHEN they actually became a Christian.

When a child believes he is a Christian but cannot articulate the exact moment he became one, you can help him remember the time by asking questions. Sometimes children will select the date of their birthday that year and claim that date. If a child is not saved, you can use the time to gently give a Gospel presentation.

Junior:
Bring in donuts or donut holes. Talk about why "Life without Jesus is like a donut," a concept developed by Rob Evans, the Donut Man. A Donut Man tape or video would be a fun thing to do for part of each birthday Sunday. (See the appendix for an address.) Take a few minutes on a birthday day to simply enjoy your students in a more informal setting. Let them share a favorite comic or a book. You may want to invest in one of the books of cartoons on church life. You may want to make an overhead of a cartoon on church life. Let the students discuss it as they enjoy the birthday donuts.

D—Develop relationships.
We live in a society where time is a precious commodity. If you feel a student needs some special relationship-building time, you may want to prayerfully consider a home visit or taking a child out for ice-cream. I have found that even asking a child to accompany you on errands can work. Children simply want time with you. You can chat and get to know each other while you are attending to your business as well.

E—Encourage your students.
Children need encouragement, even if the best we can do is to encourage the effort. It's a start. Children can handle honesty, and many are not aware their behavior may be disruptive. A gentle talk in private about misbehavior and stating what you want them to do may improve their behavior.

Children often hear what NOT to do, but we forget to tell them what TO DO. Instead of "Don't hit. Don't interrupt. Don't get off your chair," let's try some positive statements:
- "You *may* use your hands to love."
- "You *may* listen when someone else is talking. Raise your hand and then when I call on you, you may talk."
- "You *may* sit on your chair until I invite you to get up to go to the next activity."

For some children especially the doers, talkers, and touchers, these things are difficult. When they try, let's ENCOURAGE THE EFFORT:

- "I like the way you are finding more ways to show love with your hands."
- "I like the way you are trying to remember to wait to talk until I call on you."
- "I like the way you are trying to remember to sit on your chair."

F—Find something to praise each child for each Sunday.
I said this at a teacher's convention and someone said, "I have a student about whom the only positive thing I can say is, 'I sure am glad you don't go home with me.' " We laugh at this, but we have all experienced the same feeling at some time with a child. For these situations I pray silently: "Lord, help! I can't find something positive to say." He never lets me down. Something will happen in which I can sincerely praise a child.

Two teachers in a church can be so different in this area of nurturing and encouraging. One may talk about "how bad or how wild or how tough each class is" or about "all the PROBLEM children in that class." The next grade's teacher may see each child as "precious in His sight." Within weeks those "terrible problem children" may become more loving and gentle because the teacher has cultivated the positive in each child. There is power in our words, and words of encouragement can cause others to blossom and grow. Words that are hurtful cause children to close up.

G—Give awards or notes.
Carry some 3 × 5 notecards and a package of stickers with you. When a student does something for which you have been praying, shows progress in an area, or simply needs to know that you care, jot him a quick note and hand it to him on his way out of the classroom. I also use stickers and hug coupons frequently.

H—Home visits.
We live in a busy society and in many churches home visits may not be common. But they can be one of the most power-

ful ways of enhancing our ministry. We can quickly get a window into a child's life when we visit his home. Even if a family puts their best foot forward, we can still understand his home life. This can give us deeper insight on reaching him for Christ.

I—Importance of children.
In the Old as well as New Testament we see the importance of children. Our Savior also showed us that children are important and should be given attention. Can we do no less than the same?

I will stop here with my ABCs of Nurturing. I'm sure you can think of many examples to fill out the rest of the alphabet.

Nurturing Different Kinds of Learners

Our students' needs for nurturing may vary greatly based upon their homes, personalities, and life experiences. Here are a few guidelines to help us find ways to nurture different kinds of learners.

Looker
- Smile.
- Make eye contact.
- Use notes, birthday cards, attendance charts.

Talker
- Verbally affirm them.
- Let them talk and you listen.
- Talk with them.

Toucher
- Touch them.
- Let them have your physical presence near them.
- Give pats and hugs.

Doer
- Do things with them.
- Let them do things for others.
- Give them positive opportunities to DO as part of the learning time and affirm their DOING.

Fact Finder
- Give them opportunities to do objective things and praise them for things, such as being in charge of the attendance chart.
- Provide opportunities for them to do things in which you can easily praise their successes, such as Sword drills.
- Play a Bible Trivia game with them and enjoy the fact that they will probably beat you!

Nurturing Special Children

Under this canopy of nurturing, I would like to address the issue of teaching children with special needs. I am well aware that I may violate some people's comfort zones, but I feel strongly about this issue. Twenty years ago I taught multi-handicapped children. I wanted to open a special home-school environment for them where they could be trained in home living skills as well as learn some sheltered skills. I was turned down by the state because I was "too young." The Lord used this closed door to have me incorporate some of these children into the "normal" education system.

Yes, it is difficult. Yes, many people are uncomfortable. But, yes, I do believe it is necessary.

When I see an autistic child say, "Jesus" and reach out to a Sunday School teacher, I know it's right. When I see a blind child memorize perfectly with music, I know it's right. When I see "rough and tumble" boys comfort a cerebral-palsy child through a seizure, placing a stick in his mouth so he won't bite himself or choke, and change his clothes, I know it's right.

Yes, there are many days when the autistic child is loud

and disruptive, the blind child knocks over a chair, the crippled child has an accident in the middle of the room and the Down's syndrome child stubbornly won't move.

But if we teach God's love, and we teach kindness and compassion, we had better live it. The more we expose children to unusual needs, the more understanding and compassionate they become. They won't pull back because of fear of the unknown; they will embrace these differences. Isn't that, after all, Christianity in action?

I love and respect Joni Eareckson Tada tremendously. She told me people sometimes treat physically handicapped persons as if they were of lesser intelligence. How this must hurt. We are each handicapped in some way. We must learn to love and accept each other as God created us.

My brother-in-law, Dennis Dordigan, contracted multiple sclerosis during his last year at Dallas Theological Seminary and is now completely confined to a wheelchair. He was a powerful preacher when he was in prime physical condition; but he is even more powerful now, even though his voice quavers, and his wife has to look up the passages for him. Why? Because he honors God with his attitude and teaching. He could be a bitter, disillusioned, broken man. But when you see him, hear him teach, witness one of the many monologues that he has written and dramatizes, you see the Lord Jesus. He writes songs about joy. When you meet Dennis, you meet the joy in the Cross and true joy amidst the suffering. When I am having a pity party over my minor physical afflictions, I am reminded of Dennis or Joni and I am humbled. It is the testimonies of great people like these in the Kingdom from whom I want children to learn.

Treasured Teacher Training

1. What do you believe about children's needs for nurturing?

_____

_____

2. What do you believe is appropriate nurturing for the chil dren you teach?

_____

_____

3. Find evidence in the Bible of the ways Jesus loved children. List verses that show how He demonstrated this nurturing on each level:

Physical _____

_____

Emotional _____

_____

Mental _____

_____

Spiritual _____

_____

4. List ways that you can nurture your students more effectively on each level:

Physical _____

_____

Emotional _____

_____

Mental _____

_____

Spiritual _____

_____

5. Select a nurturing activity from the list and show how you are going to incorporate it into your classroom next Sunday.

_____

_____

_____

_____

_____

_____

_____

6. List three affirming verbalizations that you are going to use next Sunday.

A _____

B _____

C _____

7. What do you believe about children with special learning needs?

_____

_____

_____

_____

_____

_____

8. Write a prayer for yourself in the area of nurturing.

_____

_____

_____

Caring Communication

A Treasured Teacher is a caring communicator who provides a learning climate that helps children grow in character, content, and conduct.

"Death and life are in the power of the tongue, and those who love it will eat its fruit" (Proverbs 18:21).

The teaching objective of this chapter is to learn to be a caring communicator, who provides a learning climate that cultivates positive self-esteem and Christ-like character.

Chapter Six

In order to communicate God
we need to get close to people,
understand their needs, fears and
hopes and dreams, and then start
at that point and preach Jesus
to them, putting the story
into words and illustrations
they can understand.[1]

Leighton Ford

We were on a field trip and the children were discussing where they were born. Samantha said, "Jay was born in Miami." To which Jamie responded, "Come on, was Jay really born in 'her ami'?"

This story illustrates with delightful humor the communication chaos we create with language. Communication skills are essential with children because they do not have a complete grasp of the language, and many words are very confusing. Because they are such multi-sensory learners, we need to realize that they are often hearing us on many levels. Let's examine the various ways we can communicate with our students.

Characteristics of a Caring Communicator

Channel of love
A Treasured Teacher is a channel of God's love. His love gives us grace to love in tough situations that otherwise leave us feeling anything but loving. It grieves me to see a brilliant Bible teacher unable to truly impact his students with his message simply because he could not love them. On the other hand, I have seen lay teachers turn lives around with their simple teaching. What is that special ingredient? It is, in part, the degree of love that the teacher feels for the students. If we do not send our message bathed in love and prayer, our words may remain hollow at the podium. Love is the glue that bonds the teacher and his teaching to the student.

Characteristic of Christ
A Treasured Teacher communicates in a way that is characteristic of Jesus. If we ask ourselves, "What would Jesus say?" we sometimes learn the wisest thing to do is nothing until we feel the Lord's leading. Many times I have prayed to be "muzzle-mouthed" (Ps. 39:1) until I felt the Lord leading me. I have learned that my mouth will often get me into trouble. Jesus made every word count in His teaching. He spoke with wisdom, clarity, and love. He used examples from everyday life to make His message applicable to His students.

A Christian is . . .
A mind
through which Christ THINKS
A voice
through which Christ SPEAKS
A heart
through which Christ LOVES
A hand
through which Christ HELPS.[2]

Charged with the Holy Spirit

A Treasured Teacher, charged with the Holy Spirit, is one who allows the Holy Spirit to help him with communication. Instead of becoming frustrated with a child, we do the Christian's version of "counting to ten." Moving slowly, speaking softly, and responding gently gives the Holy Spirit a chance to work through us.

Consideration

A Treasured Teacher is one who is caring and considerate of his students. It saddens me to see teachers use their position as a podium for power. They somehow feel that their title gives them the right to "call the shots as they see them." Many a child's self-esteem has been crushed by a teacher who did not communicate positively.

I challenge you to put on a tape recorder or have someone listen to you teach and honestly appraise your communication. We may be unaware of simple things. For example, I worked hard to eliminate the "you knows" from my speaking. A year later, as I listened to a tape of myself, I was amazed at all the "you knows" that had returned in full force. This isn't a destructive communication flaw, simply an annoying one. If harmless flaws creep in, it is safe to assume that others can as well. We all have verbiage in our memory banks that we are not aware is there. Sometimes words will come out unconsciously or under pressure. Let's be careful to eliminate any words that could hurt a student.

Teachers are a walking "Show and Tell." Children are born mimics; they observe and emulate. They copy what they see modeled for them. I have seen repeatedly that a gentle, quiet teacher will have a class of gentle, quiet students. Children often live up or down to our perceptions of them.

**Children are contagious
to character and conduct.**

Clean and concise

Because children think in concrete terms, a Treasured Teacher must be clear and concise in her communication.

In discussing how to give our hearts to God for His service, each child was asked what he would like to give to God. Jamie promptly responded with "a knife." Knowing this child to be a deep thinker the teacher continued, "Why a knife, Jamie?" "So He could cut a hole through the clouds to see me better." I have learned to never underestimate the power of a child's logic.

Many words in our English language can be confusing, especially to the concrete thinking of a child. We sang a song in chapel with the words, "The presence of God watches over me." Upon leaving the chapel, one little guy asked when he was going to get his "present from God . . . you know, the 'watch' we sang about." When you sing "Our God reigns . . ." every child looks out the window to see if God is really 'raining' or not. One child described Promotion Sunday as "Commotion Sunday," and most of the teachers agreed. Yes, words can be confusing.

Words can build bridges in understanding one another, or they can create walls that keep us from understanding one another. As teachers, we are in the communication business. We need to master clear communication skills.

Dr. Howard Hendricks, a gifted communicator, writes, "The word communication comes from the Latin word 'communis,' meaning 'common.' Before we can communicate we must establish commonness, commonality. And the greater the commonality, the greater the potential for communication."[3] As teachers we must find out what is important to our children and use that as a bridge into their world.

I was teaching school in Mexico. One day I decided to teach my fifth-graders a song in English about the parts of the body. The words were fairly simply and there were corresponding actions. Later I was called to the principal's office and was asked what I was teaching the students. I sang the song for him, and he began to laugh. The simple word "knees" in the English language was a slang word in Spanish that apparently did not mean anything very edifying.

For some children our words don't communicate at all. A child visiting her grandparents attended church for the first time. Her grandfather asked what the sermon was about. "I don't know, Grandpa. He didn't say." A lot of us may be talking, but not saying anything.

Complimenting

A Treasured Teacher compliments. Let's remember to praise our students, not just for results, but for effort. When we look for things to praise in our students, it's amazing how much we find. I have seen children completely turn around in their behavior because of a teacher who cared and took time to compliment his students. There is power in praise.

**If you are having trouble finding
something to praise in a child,
pray about it. Write the child's
name on a 3 × 5 note card.
Carry it with you or post it
in a strategic place.
The Lord WILL reveal to you
something for which
to sincerely praise that child.**

Concerned

A Treasured Teacher is concerned for the personal needs of each student. In the chapter on "How Children Learn" we saw how individualized learning is. It is easy for a teacher to view the class as a whole, but if we want to transform lives for Jesus Christ, we need to reach the individual student.

As we get to know our students as individuals we find out what is important to them. This is often a key to their opening up and becoming the unique individual God meant them to be.

Children need the following components to develop positive self-esteem:

Part of

Children need to feel connected to something bigger than themselves. Because many children come from broken homes, being part of the class may be the only way they have to satisfy this need. I think the increase in gangs today is due to a growing number of kids who need to feel a part of something; gangs may be the only avenue they see as possible.

You can help your students feel a PART of something bigger than themselves.

• If they are saved, remind them of the fact that they are an integral part of the family of God. They are a child of their Heavenly Father who loves them very much.

• Always greet them by name and be happy to see them. (If you sincerely are not, and we have all been there at some time with some child, pray for God to help you with this. He will! Be ready for the blessing.)

• Hang a picture of each child in the room with a clever caption that you or the class has thought of to describe your class (i.e., First Class, Second to None, Bible Booster, Salvation Express). A class name gives students a sense of belonging.

• Extend the perimeters of the above idea to include the name of their department, their church, and their denomination. This may not seem important for some children but can be vitally important for those who need a sense of belonging.

• Let students record their attendance on a chart and offer awards for good attendance. Send an absent child a postcard saying, "We sure missed you, Jimmy. We pray that you will be back next week." A phone call and/or home visit may be a much needed link with some of these children who are drifting with little parental support at home.

Position

Children need to feel that they are special to someone. Ideally they want to feel that they are number one with someone.

• God created each of us as a very special and important individual in His kingdom. Parents help us feel this specialness. Many children do not have anyone who is lifting them up as important. When we greet each child by name, look into his eyes and find something positive to say about him, we are helping him to feel important and special. He does have an important POSITION somewhere in life.

• Sometimes a child sees his parent(s) merely as the one(s) who feeds him or tells him to go to bed. He may never go somewhere or have a heart-to-heart discussion with an adult who thinks he is really a special person. You, the Sunday School teacher, may be that special person. It was a Sunday School teacher who made Howard Hendricks feel that he had a special POSITION somewhere, and that resulted in his coming to know the Lord. Another Sunday School teacher invested time in some street boys—eight out of ten later went into full-time Christian service. One person can have a powerful impact in the life of a child. Pray to see if there is a child in your life who needs you to invest in him.

Power

Children need to feel that they have some power and can contribute in some way. This does not deny the sovereignty of God; it simply means we show children they have the power to affect their environment. For example, if a child is negative and we continue to reinforce that, we will perpetuate it. If we praise a student's effort to improve, our comments serve as a catalyst for positive changes. A child then sees that he has power to affect others' perceptions of him.

• When I was a school principal we had a student with very low self-esteem. Hal was so hungry for love, but went about getting it in all the wrong ways. As a result he had few, if any, friends.

When my children were babies, I kept them in my office until they were old enough to attend school. The students in grades 5-9 liked to get their work done quickly in study period or eat their lunch quickly and baby-sit for me. One day Hal asked if he could take Christopher. I hesitated and then suggested that we take him for a walk together. I showed him how to hold Christopher properly and the basics of caring for a little one. This same child who had often been rough with his peers became a pillar of gentleness. Christopher responded very positively to Hal, who quickly became a favorite of his.

Hal finished his work quickly each day so he could take Christopher for a while. Christopher often sought out Hal as well. Hal felt that he made a difference in someone's life. As a result, Hal's self-esteem improved greatly. He became more loving and gentle with the other students. Instead of trying to find POWER by being a bully, he found true POWER in being a gentle, loving and caring person.

• Look closely to see what a child is good at and build on that strength. You don't want to encourage competitiveness with children, but need to help each find his particular POSI-

TION in the class. This gives students a sense of the positive use of POWER in which we utilize God-given strengths to make a difference in the world. I tell children, "Each of us is really good at something and really lousy at something. Sometimes it takes years to find what we are really good at, so we need to keep on trying new things. Eventually we will discover our strengths." Like adults, children focus on their weaknesses, and that leaves us feeling powerless to make a difference in our world. A child may not realize who he is in Jesus Christ and assess his self-worth by others' perceptions. When you believe in a child and communicate that to him, you have created an island of security for him. He will want to come back to that each week. A Sunday School teacher may be the only safe island that a child has.

Amy was in my 6th grade class. She was very quiet the day we studied the passage from Romans on spiritual gifts. After class I asked if she would help me get my things back to my car. I asked her what she thought about class. She teared up. We sat in my car and had a long talk. Amy never realized that God created people differently for His special purposes. She had always felt second-best compared to her out-going sister, and as a result often retreated. She asked me what I thought her spiritual gift might be. I told her I thought she would make a marvelous teacher. She lit up. "Yes," she responded, "I have always dreamed of being a teacher." That summer I encouraged Amy to be a teacher-helper with preschoolers for Vacation Bible School. The rest is history.

Peers

We all need to feel that our peers, at least some of them, care for us and appreciate us. Many lonely children feel that no one appreciates or even notices them. Our affirmation of them in the classroom can help their peers notice something positive as well. This may backfire, and you must handle peer relationships with sensitivity and care. A teacher can create an atmosphere conducive to caring communication between students by simply not allowing them to talk negatively to or about each other. If the teacher sets this climate, the children will eventually respond.

• When I was principal, I had a rule that children were NOT allowed to speak unkindly to each other. If they did, they had to apologize. They weren't always sincere, but it was a start. If it continued, there would be appropriate punishment. Our students were not perfect angels, but they were expected to be kind to one another. When they graduated from our school I often received feedback about how kind our students were. Caring CAN be contagious.

● We can make a significant impact on our students by providing role models. The president of a Bible college said the most significant thing his parents did for him, after leading him to Christ, was to provide role models of men and women who lived the Christian faith. By observing these people, he formulated a strong Christian worldview which has sustained him through his life.

● Look around your church and community. If you teach boys, find successful athletes who know the Lord and are willing to share their testimonies. What an impact that can make upon your boys! If you teach girls, find women who are content in their role as a wife and mother. Find women who are content in being single because that is what they believe God has called them to. Have missionaries share their testimonies. Continually connect your students with people whose lives truly shine with the love of Jesus.

Positive Experiences

Positive experiences build on each other. A teacher saying, "I believe in you" can be the first step on the road to many positive experiences.

It is natural to want to feel good. We all want to enjoy the positive experiences of feeling loved, affirmed, encouraged, and supported. The church can provide this kind of supportive environment for children. Children will want to come back, time and time again. (See chapter 8 for specific suggestions.)

Credible

Children have an antenna for authenticity. They can sense when adults are being "real" with them. If children believe we are genuine in what we say, they will "buy" into other things we share. Likewise, if they believe we have deceived them, they may not see any of what we are sharing as credible. Credibility always precedes communication.

Convicted

If we are convicted of our unworthiness to teach and are likewise convicted of our great worth through Christ, we will be transformed teachers. Because children can sense credibility, they can learn much from the testimony of our lives.

Consistent

Consistency is one of the most important qualities a teacher has in dealing with children. According to them, one of the most valued qualities in teachers is "fairness." Part of fairness is consistency. We must be consistent in our walk and in our talk. Our lives must be a genuine reflection of what we teach the children.

Compassionate

Let us be compassionate with our children. This doesn't mean that we are softies who accept their hangnail that prevented them from doing their homework. It means we truly try to empathize with what they are going through. Childhood can be a very challenging and traumatic time. To hear, "Oh come on, what's wrong with you? Don't you know these are the best years of your life?" may cause them not to want the rest of their lives. Before we judge a child, let us pray that we understand what living that child's life would be like.

Communication Caricatures

Communication, like everything else, is an individualized experience. Our personalities, learning processes, and patterns come into play. How we "hear" something that is being communicated to us may well be affected by our learning style. Rarely do two people hear something in quite the same way. The following are communication suggestions for the lively learners we have in our class.

Lookers
The Spoken Word

LOOKERS, as a general rule, notice body language. They may hear what your body is saying more than they hear your words. This underscores the need for consistency between our walk and our talk. They respond best to words consistent with their learning style:

- "I am LOOKING to SEE who is sitting quietly."
- "I SEE that you found your Bible."
- "LOOK into your Bible and SEE what God has to say about obeying your parents."

Body Language
LOOKERS respond positively to visual body language clues:
- Smile
- Direct eye contact
- Body language that communicates love and joy, rather than anger and frustration. LOOKERS say things like, "Are you upset with me?"

Environmental Communication
LOOKERS like their learning environment orderly and attractive. They notice when the teacher brings order and creativity to the classroom. As a teacher who is LOOKER, I LOOK for ways to make the room as attractive as possible. Some children seem oblivious to this, but LOOKERS always respond positively to changes and additions in the physical environment. LOOKERS often have very strong responses to their environment and prefer it orderly and quiet. Teachers need to respect and protect this, as well as to train LOOKERS in tolerance and adaptability.

My son is a LOOKER and notices when I have done something to his room. He also spends time on his room getting it just the way he likes it. I as a LOOKER need to have my physical environment just the way I like it before I can concentrate. I find I cannot work with sound. Piano lessons were conducted right next to my office. I love music, but I quickly learned I could not work effectively with distractions. I did other things on piano-lesson day like purchasing supplies and cleaning the resource room.

Talkers
The Spoken Word
TALKERS respond well to words that are consistent with their learning style.
- "I HEAR what you are SAYING."
- "I am LISTENING for people who are remembering our rules."

Body Language
TALKERS hear the slightest change in your oral communication. This child hears irritation in your voice. A paradox with this learner is that he processes what he is learning by hearing it and talking about it. In fact, TALKERS often generate noise, but do not respond well to noise from others.

Environmental Communication
TALKERS like to have some sound in the environment and will often create it, such as humming. Providing "white noise," such as soft classical music, or allowing him to sit by something that hums like an air-conditioning unit or computer, will help him.

Our oldest is a talker. He likes to study with music. He often talks loudly and more frequently than many would like, yet he is very intolerant of others creating noise. When the dog barks or his siblings play the piano, he is the first to be distracted. The dilemma is to help him learn tolerance of others while not creating so much noise himself.

Touchers
The Spoken Word
TOUCHERS definitely need physical touch, and there aren't as many words that communicate this as easily as the first two. Words that TOUCHERS "hear" are:

● "I am TOUCHED by what you have said."

● "HOLD that thought and we will discuss it some more."

● "You may follow along with your FINGER as I read this to you."

● "You may get something from the shelf or a center and learn more about our lesson by DOING the puzzle, felt lesson or . . ."

Body Language
Touch is definitely the arena in which you reach this learner. We have to be particularly sensitive to the appropriateness of how we touch. Frequently passing by this child helps a great deal. Love pats encourage him and a firm hand on the shoulder (but do not hurt or pinch please!) help tremendously to keep the TOUCHER in line.

Because he needs touch to such a great extent, the

TOUCHER has a great deal of trouble keeping his hands off others. He needs constant reminders that "We keep our hands on our own body unless we have permission." The best way to avoid problems is to have something in a TOUCHER's hands as often as possible to "keep him busy."

Environmental Communication
Having things in the classroom for a child to touch becomes an emotional security blanket for a TOUCHER. Because he is always "fiddling," a TOUCHER often receives the message that he is annoying people. He is simply responding in his own learning style and doesn't understand WHY he does what he does, and that it can be irritating. He needs to be given permission to as well as demonstration of, appropriate touching in order to learn.

I substituted in a class where there was nothing for the children to touch. A definite TOUCHER was disturbing all of us. I put him by me and tried to give him plenty of touches and allowed him to play with my hand. As I got ready to present the Gospel, I took off my necklace and gave it to him to touch. When these learners are older, we can help them understand their need for touch and give them appropriate ways to touch when there is nothing in the environment. Instead of "fiddling," this child can doodle on paper.

Doers
The Spoken Word
DOERS are so action-oriented that they respond best to words that have lots of action in them.
- "We will DO the lesson now."
- "SHOW me that you are ready for me to teach you."
- "FOLD your hands and TURN your eyes to me so I can see that you are ready."
- "I need for you to SHOW me that you can listen as I explain this and then I will let you DO something that shows me that you understand the lesson."

Body Language
DOERS are children on the move. You as the teacher need to be on the move, as well. When you rotate around the classroom, they do better. The more things you can give them to

do, the more you can effectively direct their busy bodies. Let a DOER collect papers, pass out markers, erase the board, and do anything else he can do physically.

Environmental Communication
DOERS definitely respond best to a centers approach (see chapter 11). The DOER needs to believe he will get a chance to DO something. Include drama in your presentation. You may simply have a box of old bathrobes and towels, and say to this child, "Would you like to act this out for us?" He will welcome anything that you allow him to DO. Remember, a DOER learns when his body is in movement; the more you can allow him to DO the better.

I never cease to be amazed at how consistent these learners are. In group time they can be annoying as they get up, lean back on their chairs, bother the person next to them, or other inappropriate behaviors. When you give them something to DO, they are incredibly focused and easy to manage.

Fact Finders
The Spoken Word
FACT FINDERS think in terms of black and white. They only think they are learning when they are being presented with and taught factual, objective information. The more you talk to them in this particular language, the more they will relate to you.

- "HOW MANY disciples were there?"
- "WHAT TIME did Jesus die on the cross?"
- "WHAT IS the difference between a scribe and a Pharisee?"
- "WHERE did Jesus perform His first miracle?"
- "WHAT is the rule in our classroom about . . ."
- "HOW MANY students are present today?"
- "WHAT TIME does this class end?"

Body Language
FACT FINDERS are more serious and prefer a more academic teacher. Somehow they take you more seriously when you have a book (preferably the Bible!) in your hand and you do the traditional teaching tasks such as lecture, write on the board, and present factual information.

Environmental Communication

They like to have resources that are of a factual nature. FACT FINDERS like reference books, maps, and charts. They do not do well with subjective discussions or drama. They want the facts and only the facts! They prefer a very academically-oriented environment.

Communication As a Bridge or a Roadblock

Communication can be a bridge to facilitate the teaching process or it can be a roadblock. There are certain communication principles that hold true in any teaching situation, and there are some communication tools that work best with each individual learner. The following diagram serves to illustrate general communication principles that build or block the teaching process. Prayerfully examine your own communication to see where your teaching lies. Ask God to help you see and/or hear how your communication impacts your students.

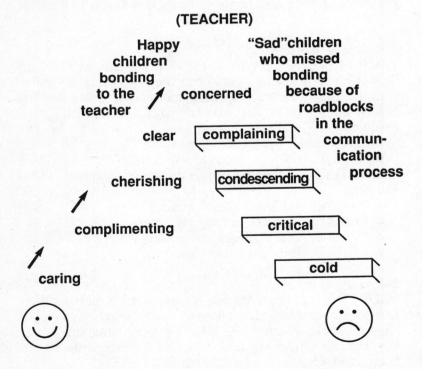

98

Treasured Teacher Training
1. Take a minute to evaluate your communication skills.
Give yourself a score for each item below.
   3: You feel that you communicate this well.
   2: You are average; some days you do this well and other days you "blow it."
   1: This is an area in which you need improvement.

_____ CARING

_____ CONSIDERATE

_____ CLEAR AND CONCISE

_____ CREDIBLE

_____ COMPASSIONATE

_____ CONSISTENT

_____ CONCERNED

TOTAL: _____

Looking at your score thus far:

18-21: You are a caring considerate communicator. Praise the Lord and continue communicating well.

10-17: You are progressing. The following bridge-building exercise may help you to incorporate more bridge-builders in your communication.

4-9: Communication is an area to be in prayer about. God will honor your desire to be a more effective communicator and will help you.

1-3: Whoops! Time for a real concerted effort to improve.

2. Now score yourself on these criteria:
   3: You do this frequently.
   2: You do this sometimes.

1: You rarely exhibit this quality.

_____ CRITICAL

_____ CONDESCENDING

_____ CONTROLLED

_____ COLD

_____ COMPLAINING

_____ CONFUSING

_____ COARSE, CRUDE

TOTAL _____

18-21:   Whoops! Time to make some changes. Hit the floor on your knees!

11-17:   Stay on your knees. Begin making a list of the words you want to eliminate from your communication. Pray about one and begin a serious campaign to eliminate it. After that one is gone, begin another.

4-12:   You are doing OK. Pray to get better.

1-3:   You are doing super! Praise the Lord and keep it up!

3. In the following diagram, list words that you feel you are now using as bridge builders on the right side. Then list the words that you want to incorporate on the left bridge. These will serve as reminders of words that you want to communicate with as a Treasured Teacher.

4. On the top roadblock, list words that you feel you use now that you want to eliminate. Write them down and then put a big red X through them. On the roadblock on the bottom, write a Scripture verse over the roadblock that you're going to commit to memory to help you be a more effective communicator.

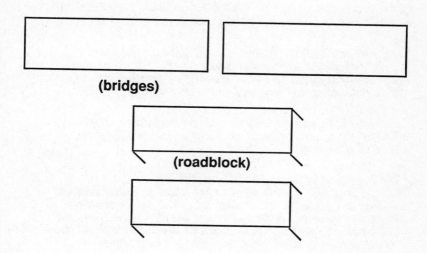

(bridges)

(roadblock)

1 Corinthians 13 for Teachers

When I published my Christian Time Organizers, my dear friend Sue Bohlin wrote and calligraphied this for the organizers. It is such a blessing and I want to share it with you.

1 Corinthians 13 for Teachers

If I converse eloquently in "educationalese" and "parent-ese" but have not love, I am only a fire-drill blast or end-of-day bell.

If I can intuit what my students will grow up to be, and if I understand all the scope and sequence charts, and if my confidence in my students' abilities produces all positive self-fulfilling prophecies, but have not love, I am a zero.

If I buy shoes and clothing for my poorer students, or if I volunteer for an inner city combat-zone school, but have not love, I've done it all for nothing.

Love is graciously helping a slow student "get it." Love is finding something kind to say to every child and never allowing any child to be laughed at. It does not get miffed when other teachers are given the better equipment and facilities; it does not gloat when one's test scores are 30 points above the national norm; it is not arrogant about clearly superior teaching skills.

Love does not rudely interrupt a child; it is not on a power trip; it does not explode when shown disrespect; it does not keep a secret column of grudges in the record book.

Love hates it when children are caught in the fallout of evil choices, and delights when they choose honesty. It always shields children from things that would cause them to grow up too soon, always builds trustworthiness by giving children opportunities to be trusted, always believes the best about students, always stays with people and projects to the end.

Love will never be unsuccessful, as God views success.

But where there are intuitions, they will cease; where there is educational jargon, that will be stilled; where there are scope and sequence charts, they will pass away.

Now these three remain: seeing the potential in a child with the eyes of faith, believing the best about a child with the will of hope, and seeking the highest good for a child with the heart of love.

But the greatest of these is love.—

Paraphrased & Lettered
by Sue Bohlin

102

Desirable Discipline

A Treasured Teacher understands the process of discipline and practices desirable discipline.

"All discipline for the moment seems not to be joyful, but sorrowful; yet to those who have been trained by it, afterwards it yields the peaceful fruit of righteousness" (Hebrews 12:11).

The teaching objective of this chapter is to learn to discipline students effectively.

Chapter Seven

**No horse gets anywhere until
he is harnessed. No steam or gas
ever drives anything until it is
confined. No Niagara is ever
turned into light and power until
it is tunneled. No life ever grows
great until it is focused, dedicated,
disciplined.[1]**

This chapter is designed to help you learn to discipline effectively. I thought that if you loved children and you loved the Lord, you could go into a classroom, share your message, and everything would be great. I spent quite a few nights in tears trying to figure out why it wasn't working. In the process, I learned things about discipline that work. My prayer is that they will work for you.

Dedicate Teaching to the Glory of God
We must always remember why we are teaching. We are there for the Lord. We are not there to win a popularity

contest or to see who is the best at discipline. Let's keep our focus on Him. So we begin by dedicating our teaching to the glory of God.

Demonstrate the love of Christ

We must learn what it means to demonstrate the love of Christ. We must first know Him personally as Lord and Savior of our lives. Second, we must demonstrate His gentleness as well as His strength. This combination will make you a good disciplinarian.

Dominance of the Holy Spirit

As believers in Jesus Christ, we receive the gift of the Holy Spirit. He will help us to know what to say, as well as when we need to be quiet. Children are used to adults "becoming frustrated" with discipline and can often "punch our buttons" quickly. Praying for help from the Holy Spirit is the Christian version of counting to ten. Instead of *reacting* on the human level, we *respond* from Spirit.

One way to rely on the Spirit when disciplining is to walk and talk as if in slow motion. Walk slowly to a child requiring discipline. If your eyes are on him, all eyes will be on you. As you walk, pray. You will find your response more appropriate because you have placed yourself under the *leading* of the Holy Spirit.

Instead of disciplining a student by yelling across the room, try the following:

1. Keep your eyes on the child.
2. Walk slowly to the child, keeping your eyes on him at all times.
3. As you walk, pray for the Holy Spirit to control your attitude and actions.
4. When you get to the child, put your face next to his and look into his eyes.
5. If he will not give you eye contact, gently cup his face in your hand and put your face even closer. Some children may look away and others may close their eyes to avoid looking at you. Because eye contact is so important, wait it out. When you get the eye contact, state your desire, "In my classroom, you may use your hands to

love or create or work; you may NOT use them to hurt.
Do you understand?"
6. As you walk away, walk backward, keeping your eyes
   on the child.
7. Calmly continue teaching.

The calmer and more deliberate you appear, the better
your ability to achieve the desired result and the more sensitive you will be to the leading of the Holy Spirit.

Define your discipline style

It is very important that we model the behavior we expect
from our students. If we arrive late to class, interrupt, talk
rudely, or lack self-control, then we can expect our students
to exhibit the same behaviors. We model the appropriate
behaviors we expect from our students. Our students learn
more from what we are than from what we say. If you teach
young children, you can often see your teaching behaviors
mimicked by observing students playing "teacher." This can
be painful if you aren't ready to deal with truth or face aspects of your teaching which you are unaware of or unwilling
to change.

Be diligent in your preparation

The more diligent we are in our preparation, the fewer discipline problems we will have. Children can always sense when
we are not prepared, and they may try to take advantage of
us.

When we rush into class at the last minute without all our
supplies, frantically trying to find and set up materials, we
invite children to misbehave, especially the "one child that
can fill up the entire room." You can count on that child to be
there early the day you are running late. This child is "everywhere," and the others respond to him. The result is confusion and chaos.

Contrast this scenario with one in which you are demon-
strating diligent preparation. You arrive before the children,
set up the room, organize your visuals and craft supplies, and
you are calm, collected, and composed. You greet each child
at the door. You are in control and your teaching is more
effective.

Proper Planning Produces Positive Performances

Developmental foresight
We need to take time to study about the children we will teach. Knowing what a two-year-old or a twelve-year-old is like helps us to have realistic expectations and to teach age-appropriately.

Sometimes a teacher thinks a child is a child is a child, and teaching one age means he can teach another. That is not true. Each age has its own distinctive characteristics. Here is a brief description of each age (and there are many!):

● Two-year-olds are trying to assert their independence.

● Three-year-olds are not sure they want to grow up, and can be somewhat clingy and whiny.

● Four-year-olds are out of bounds! Everything is too extreme: they laugh too hard, cry too hard, play too hard, and think that bathroom words are really funny.

● Five-year-olds adore you. If you want to be loved, this is the age to teach. They think their teacher is the center of their little universe. Perhaps God in His wisdom made five-year-olds to follow four-year-olds so we wouldn't get too discouraged.

● Six-year-olds are very emotional, talkative, and somewhat aggressive. They can be a challenge to discipline because they are trying to achieve their independence again.

● Seven-year-olds are beginning some internal reflection and can be more pensive and ready for more subjective concepts. They can also withdraw, complain, and whine and may need extra encouraging.

● Eight-year-olds rush out to meet the world. While the eight-year-old is asserting his independence again, he is also very dependent upon the approval of significant adult figures in his life. They want approval so much that they study your every response. They may have excessive demands for attention, affection, and appropriate (by his definition) responses from you.

● Nine-year-olds seek approval from peers more than from adults. They very much want to be in control of their world and resist too much adult interference. They may be slow to obey, not so much out of defiance, but in order to feel that they are captains of their own ship. Outwardly, they may appear independent, but inside they worry about things. This worrying may manifest itself in a great deal of complaining.

● Ten-year-olds want to be good and do what is right. It is one of the nicest ages. Recent trends describe the ten-year-old as very moody. My personal opinion is that external influences such as television, commercials, billboards, dress, and discussions on AIDS, abortion, and sex have accelerated the developmental rate in children. Ten-year-olds often manifest signs of an early transition from child to adolescent by being moody.

The bottom line is: TAKE TIME TO STUDY WHAT IS DEVELOPMENTALLY APPROPRIATE. Your teacher guide should provide this for you. If not, suggestions for possible reading are available in the back of this chapter. KNOW THY STUDENTS!

Decide and define your basic rules
A newly-hired principal discovered that the walls of the cafeteria were covered with rules. They were so overwhelming that instead of curtailing negative behavior, the rules served as a challenge to find new and creative ways to have negative behavior slip between the cracks of two rules. Keep your rules short and simple if you want effective discipline.

I have been using three simple rules because they work and cover a broad range of behaviors. You may want to have children recite these rules to you each week.

1. Raise your hand if you want to speak, and wait to be called upon.
2. You may not talk if someone else is talking.
3. Keep your hands on your own body unless you have permission to touch someone else.

End your sentences by dropping your voice. Children don't take you seriously when you end by raising your voice. Practice talking in a lower, softer voice. You'll have far fewer discipline problems.

Develop your system based on your teaching style
Teacher, know thyself. We need to understand what works for us and stay with it. This may take some trial and error, but we will eventually find our comfort zone. We need to be authentic in how we communicate our desires to our students.

When I taught children in grades 3-6 who were auditory and often talked out of turn, I said, "I know that you need to let me know what you think, and talking is a way to express yourself. I want to allow this. However, I am a teacher who likes quiet, and I want to call on you. I am strict about noise levels. I will respect your desires, and you need to show respect for mine." Understanding why I require what I do makes a class more willing to cooperate with me.

If you are a fun-loving teacher, you will create an entirely different atmosphere than the marine sergeant. Don't compare yourself to another teacher. Do what works for you. If you see certain behaviors or classroom environments you would like to emulate, learn from them. But remember that your teaching style and temperament affects how you discipline. Be fair to yourself in accepting how God created you.

Differentiate between Consequences and Punishment
Because true discipline is a process of training in appropriate behavior, we must understand the difference between a consequence (or effect) and punishment. Children may view both as a "punishment," but we must be able to distinguish between the two. Children often say a teacher is "mean;" in reality what they are saying is that a teacher is "strict." It's good/OK to be strict. *Just be fair.* Children have an antenna for what is fair and just. A CONSEQUENCE is a FAIR response to behavior that will elicit a more appropriate future response. A PUNISHMENT is often overstated, inappropriate and creates negative future responses from the child, rather than a positive life-changing response. Let's look at several situations.

- The rule is when we make a mess we clean it up. Andy *made a big mess* in a center and went to the next center. An appropriate CONSEQUENCE is that he has to clean up the mess before he goes to the next center. A PUNISHMENT is that I bring the class' attention to the mess. I do not allow him to *participate* in any more centers for the day.

● Another rule is we raise our hands to talk during class discussion. Emily continually talks out without raising her hand. A CONSEQUENCE is that she may not talk until she raises her hand and is called on. If she does not raise her hand, she will go to the "time-out" chair; she may listen but not participate in the discussion until she is invited back to her place. A PUNISHMENT is to write 100 times on paper: "I will not interrupt."

The purposes of a consequence are to:

1. train appropriate behavior
2. preserve the child's dignity
3. increase an internal focus of responsibility
4. increase student motivation by facilitating positive self-esteem
5. show the student how to work within a system where there is give-and-take
6. help them learn cause-and-effect relationships
7. maintain a climate of caring

After we decide what our rules are, we need to decide what the consequences will be if those rules are broken; for example:

1. Sit in time-out chair
2. Lose special privileges
3. Talk to parents
4. Have to be sent out of the room

Sequence with preschoolers
Let's follow a typical sequence with a child between the ages of two and six. Let's imagine he has just hit another child. Here are some steps we can take.

1. Walk slowly and deliberately to that child. (Don't yell across the room . . . please!)

2. Get on his level, look into his eyes and say quietly, "The rule in our classroom is that we keep our hands on our own body unless we have permission."

3. Look into his eyes and firmly say, "Do you under-

109

stand?" Use eye contact to show you mean business.

4. Quietly go back to your teaching, walking backward with eyes on the child. Hopefully that will be the end of it, but let's assume it continues.

5. Walk to the child again, hold his hands, look him in the eye and quietly and firmly ask, "What is the rule in our classroom?"

6. He may or may not answer. Regardless of his response, take him to an isolated chair. This is *not* a Dummy Chair or a Bad Chair; it is a *Time-Out Chair*. Put him on the chair as you say, "The rule in our classroom is that you keep your hands on your own body. You hit Sarah, and hitting is not allowed in our classroom. You *may* sit here until *I* invite you back to join the class. I want you to look and tell me if you see anyone else hitting in our classroom."

7. If he sits there quietly, return within one or two minutes. Get on your knees, hold his hands, look into his eyes, and say, "I see that you are sitting very quietly, I am very proud of you. Tell me, did you see anyone else hitting in our classroom? We do not hit in our classroom. You may come back now."

8. If he did *not* sit there quietly, I would suggest the following:

a. He needs to sit there until he shows you, by his actions, that he can be invited to return to the classroom.
b. He loses special privileges, such as: time with a favorite activity.
c. Send a note home to his parents, or call them.

9. If the child continues to disrupt, I strongly recommend that you remove him from the classroom. If the other students see a child dominating your time and attention, they will try the same thing. I suggest having someone that can help you by taking the child out of the classroom. This may be a roving Director of Christian Education or a department head. You may have to recruit a person who is discerning, loving, and firm to check your classroom once or twice an hour to see if you need a "helping hand."

To sum up:

1. Go directly to the child and speak firmly and quietly.

2. State the rule first, giving him the benefit of the doubt. (Rule amnesia is prevalent among some children.)

3. For the next offense, he must state the rule.

4. Go to the Time-Out Chair. If he is quiet, you may invite him back within one to five minutes.

5. If he is disruptive, he must stay on the chair until he shows you he is ready to return. Being in your class is a great privilege; assume he will want to be there.

6. Talk to his parents.

7. Have the Sunday School Superintendent or someone else take him from the class if his behavior is a significant disruption. This is very important. Children must see that teaching the Word of God is our first priority, and their behavior will not deter us from that goal.

A Word to the Wise

When you talk to a parent about a child, do not show anger. Smile, approach the parent with something positive to say about the child, and then say, "I am having a little trouble with . . ." and state the problem. Then say, "I wonder if you could help me?" This is far more effective than *yanking the child up* to the parent and showing your obvious displeasure.

When you approach a parent aggressively, he has no recourse but to defend his child. He may know exactly what you are talking about, but will defend his child because you are on the offensive, or he may honestly not know what you are talking about, and will consequently defend his child. In either case, you lose.

If you approach a parent kindly and gently, with an "I" statement *("I* have a problem . . . "), the parent is much more likely to want to help. It is well worth time to make friends with your parents because they can be a tremendous help to you. If they feel you truly care about their child and want what is best for him, they will work with you.

Sequence with primary grades

For a child in grades 1-3, use the same basic sequence. For a child in grades 4-6, dignity becomes a critical issue because he cares deeply about what his peers think of him. DISCIPLINE WITH DIGNITY is important for all ages, but be especially sensitive to children between ages nine and eleven. I prefer to talk with this child after class and before the next class about his behavior, in *private*. Try to enlist him as a friend and helper. For example, I might say, "I truly am happy to be your teacher. I believe that teaching the Word of God is the most important thing I can do. Because I believe it is so important, I want to be sure that each of my students understands what I am teaching. When you make sounds, poke others, make airplanes from your lesson (or whatever else he is doing), I find it difficult to teach. I wonder if you could help me." Believe it or not, some children are NOT aware of what a disruption they are causing. This is the age to be loving, and sometimes bluntly honest. Be sure to speak to the child in private so he can "save face."

Dealing with the Difficult Child

Every church across America has at least one difficult child, and often several. It may be safe to say there is an increasing number of these children. When I do a teacher training workshop on discipline, I say to teachers, "I will be happy to teach your class for you so you can see these things demonstrated firsthand." Sometimes people take me up on this offer. Modeling is one of the most effective ways to teach. Who are some of these difficult children?

The defiant child

The defiant child is a strong-willed child who wants "control at any cost." Always look in this child's eyes. If you discern rebellion or defiance, I encourage you to take strong action. This does not mean to yell, scream, or use physical abuse, but rather be strong, controlled, and ready to require obedience on his part. Defiance is sin. Strong wills must learn submission to authority. Your manner may produce greater results than your words.

A verbalization that has worked for me with defiant children is, "I can see that you have some skills that could make you a leader. You are a very strong child. We need strong leaders in this world. God may call you to leadership some day. It is important that you first learn to follow because great leaders first learn to follow. God placed me in charge of this classroom. The Bible says we must each come under the authority of those God has placed in charge (see 1 Tim. 4:7;

Heb. 12:6). I am going to be strict with you because I want you to grow to be a godly leader whom God can use in His army."

Kids respond well to truth. Communication like this brings down a wall that exists between adults and children, teachers and students, and which children think they have to continually defy. Children respond positively when they realize that we want to work WITH them because we care.

It is up to you not to tolerate defiant behavior from this child. Be sure that you have thought through what you will and will not tolerate. Have a consequence ready for deliberate defiance.

If younger children refuse to do something, I put my body around theirs and literally "do it" with them. For children in grades K-2, I have them sit in the Time-Out Chair until they are ready to obey. I look deeply into their eyes and say, "This is unacceptable to me. I will not allow you to act in this way. Do you understand me?" Remember, there is power in eye contact and it is effective with these children. Again, always end by dropping your voice. These children, more than any others, will take advantage of you if they think you are weak and acting without conviction. Rebellion IS sin and must be dealt with strongly.

The disruptive child

The disruptive child is often a TALKER because he loves noise and often creates his own. If there is no defiance (look in his eyes if you aren't sure), but simply subconsciously, he likes noise, gently remind him to be quiet. He usually isn't aware of his disruption and just needs humor or love pats to help him remember. The TOUCHER may be disruptive because he simply needs to touch. He is driven by this need and his hands are seemingly everywhere. Get something in his hands to touch. This usually gets him doing something CONSTRUCTIVE, and you can resolve most of his disruptive behavior. Because the DOER learns when movement is felt in the muscle-tone of his body, he will be continually trying to move. If you want everyone to sit still and listen to you, you will definitely view this child as a distraction.

Most disruptive children are simply being disruptive out of their learning style, and most of the disruptive behaviors can be rerouted into more appropriate behavior. Be gentle unless you see DEFIANCE in their eyes.

I arranged "An Old-Fashioned Christmas" birthday party for my daughter's first grade class. When I wanted them to sit, listen, and participate as a class, I had to deal with disruptive behavior. When we moved to CHRISTMAS CENTERS, those that had been disruptive were now very focused, and I had no discipline problems. Afterward, my daughter and I evaluated the day. She had been my "teacher helper" since it was also her birthday. She said "Mommy, children need to move and touch. That is when they act the best." I responded with an inward smile of great joy, but to her I responded, "Honey, when you are grown up and a teacher, remember that very important pearl of wisdom that you have gleaned from today. Mommy believes that and yet I had to be reminded of that again today."

Do's and Don'ts of Discipline

Direct eye contact
Teachers, learn to use your eyes to minimize discipline problems. Our society has become depersonalized. Eyes can communicate so much. Look into the eyes of your students. Communicate that you care. Communicate that you mean business when it comes to discipline. Use your eyes to help students to feel an integral part of the class.

Diligence
Muscles become stronger with use, and so do "our discipline muscles." We must work diligently to find the plan of discipline that works for us, and we must be *consistent* in carrying it out. There is not a time when we can stop disciplining our students, but as we become more proficient and confident in our system, there comes a point at which we no longer have to think about it. It becomes second nature to us. First year teachers often lament that "all they do is discipline, they want to teach." It will come, be patient. Be diligent.

Detachment
I almost shudder as I write this because I fear being misinterpreted in this area. I am a toucher of children, and I believe in

bonding to them with love. But when it comes to discipline, the secret lies in DETACHMENT. When we don't react to the many antics children use to detour us, and we are *detached* from these actions, they begin to diminish. When we remain *detached* to their negative behavior, and are warmly, positively responsive to their positive behavior, the negative diminishes and the positive behavior increases.

The adage that says "I love you, but I don't like what you did" applies here. We DETACH ourselves from the "riff-raff" of children's antics, but we don't detach ourselves from the love and caring that we feel for them. I use humor. When they try to push my buttons, I simply raise my eyebrows with a look of mock disbelief like "Surely you are kidding me . . . you don't really want to act that way now do you?" Sometimes, you simply need to just ignore it. If you react with annoyance to each little antic, you will be like a rubber ball bouncing around all the time. Learn to RESPOND rather than REACT.

Direct your attention to the little things and the big things rarely happen
Usually teachers *let* the little things *go* and then wonder where all the big problems come from. Little things include how students sit in their chairs, chewing gum, comments made under their breaths, and poor manners.

As a teacher, I walk around. You can resolve most potential discipline problems by simply walking around and redirecting children. Don't lecture, simply redirect. I always wear something with pockets. If students play with little treasures from home, I simply pop them in my pockets. They have already been told that disruptive treasures go into my pockets and may be retrieved *after* class *with* Mom or Dad.

Insist on good manners. We live in a world that does not value good manners. As Christians, let's use good manners in our relationships with children and insist they use good manners with us.

When the class gets ready to walk in the halls, have them line up quietly. Keep wandering hands from meandering into trouble by having students fold their hands in front of them or behind their backs. This isn't legalism; it is simply orderliness.

Determine internal rather than external focus
Discipline is a PROCESS which requires on-going training. We want to train our students to be responsible for their own behavior. Teaching responsibility requires an internal focus, and children typically want to blame others instead of assuming responsibility for their own actions.

If I ask a student, "Where is your Bible?", he will usually have an external focus which draws responsibility away from himself: "My mom didn't remind me to get it." OR "We had to leave in such a hurry that I forgot," OR "You didn't tell us we had to bring our Bibles."

If clearly stated expectations are not followed, we have an excellent opportunity to help students learn an internal focus and take responsibility. Like everything else in training and disciplining children, it requires patience.

Decade of me, TV and decline of family
The focus of our society/world is on ME and little on THEE, abetted by TV and the decline of the family. The result is an ever-increasing need for discipline. For many students, the church and school are the only environments in which discipline exists. The goal of external discipline is to develop the internal self-discipline needed to be a disciple of Jesus Christ. Teachers, let us embrace this training process as unto the Lord. Proverbs 22:6 is not a PROMISE, but a PROCESS. Let us seek to "train up a child (student) in the way he should go, even when he is old he will not depart from it." This reaches far beyond the teaching hour, the perimeters of our classroom walls, and our curriculum. This is training disciplined people who are not just thinking of ME and who form their opinions from TV. These are disciples of the Lord Jesus Christ who are trained to think of others, to form their convictions from the Scriptures, and who are committed to family. Family units should train in these qualities, but realistically, it may only be coming from our teaching each Sunday.

116

When we view discipline from this perspective, we are training in skills needed for life.

Dramatize

When we teach little children, we can really dramatize. I say things in an exaggerated manner, such as: "Can you walk back to class so quietly that tomorrow the pastor will ask me, 'Did the two-year-olds come to church yesterday?' I'll tell him, 'Yes, they were here,' but he won't think so because you were *so* quiet." Children enjoy that until they reach about age four. Then you have to change it and say, "Let's see if you can walk so quietly that your teacher won't hear you come in!" I always tell the teacher ahead of time, so she will be busy with her back turned when they walk in and sit down. They sit so quietly and think they are so clever. This works! It won't work past second grade, so simply say, "You *will* walk quietly to class." Teaching little ones can be so much fun by being very dramatic.

Don't yell, use the bell

When we yell, children get louder and the noise level goes up. Get a bell with a soft tone, and make a game. You can say, "This is the Freeze Game. When you hear the bell, turn your eyes to me, hold your hands behind your back, and "freeze." After I say what I need to say, you may "defrost."

I also like to sing to the children. Singing rules or directions to them is such a change, that they will pay attention. Before I share something important I always sing, "Eyes on me by the time I count to three." I do not proceed until all eyes are on me. You can't "force" children to listen, but it certainly helps when you have their eyes focused on you.

The quieter your voice is, the quieter your classroom will be. Ask any teacher who has had laryngitis. Teachers who yell have noisy classrooms. Teachers who speak softly have quiet classrooms. The secret is that students must be quiet before you speak. Insist on it. Train them in it. It will make teaching so much more pleasant.

Deliver an interesting message

Please don't bore children. Develop a rhythm to your teaching. Teach multisensory whenever possible. Always keep

117

one step ahead of them. If something isn't working, simply move on to something else.

Display humor

I tell you to be strict, to drop your voice, to speak softly, to insist on good manners, and then I say display humor. You can display humor, but you can't do it from the start. You must first establish discipline with your students, and then you can begin to have fun. Be willing to be silly and to try new things, and if you say the wrong thing, it's OK. Children love to see you laugh at your own mistakes and say, "Whoops!" Have fun with your students. Be willing to say, "I'm sorry." That teaches tremendous lessons to our students.

Design your room

Enriched Preschool Environment

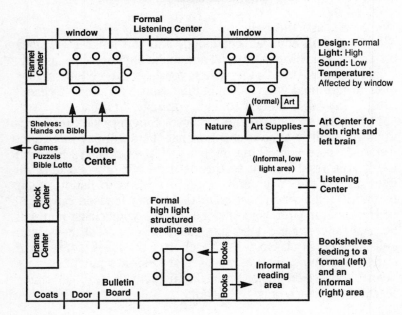

Individuals learn in different ways. Much of what we see as a discipline problem may be a student who is not in his comfort zone of learning. We do not need to pamper our learners and give them everything they want. That would simply feed the above-stated "ME" focus. However, negative discipline can be eliminated by our avoiding situations in which a child will act up. On page 118 is a Sunday School environment plan for children ages 2-7 which can prevent an abundance of distracting wiggles:

We provide quiet, structured areas for learners who need that kind of environment. More importantly, we create an environment where the TOUCHER and DOER can learn in their comfort zone more effectively. We don't use these areas the entire hour, but they are available when the need arises.

Dignify each child
Find something positive to say about each child. Stand at the door and say something positive, and hug or pat each child. We may be the only encouragement the student gets all week. If we want them to fall in love with Jesus Christ, we need to demonstrate love that is Christ in action.

Discover the beauty in each child or pray for God to reveal it to you
There are some children who are difficult to love. You may say, "I have tried and tried to find something about this child to love and I can't." Pray, get on your knees and ask the Lord to help you find something to love in this child. It is amazing what He will bring to mind or what event He will cause to happen. You may walk to your car on a rainy day, drop your papers, and that child will be right there to pick them up. Something will happen so that you can truly praise, love, and dignify that child. The Lord will orchestrate that for you if you pray about it.

Display godly qualities to the children
Can you imagine Jesus Christ yelling at a child? You know that is not what He would do. Let's not overreact when things go wrong. If your easel gets knocked over or a child spills a tub of paint, it is not the end of the world. We are

there to teach children about God. Let's take that responsibility very seriously. We want them to feel that we are prepared and that we want to teach them about the Lord.

**You teach LITTLE
by what you SAY,
but you teach MOST
by what you ARE.[2]**

Let us be more dedicated to being better disciplinarians, and we will love the process of teaching much more. Discipline is inherent to teaching. The need to discipline doesn't go away, but the time spent on it will diminish. Mastering discipline will help you become a master teacher.

Discipline is a very important aspect of teaching, and an element that can often "make or break" the teacher. Many gifted teachers have quit because they became weary of the discipline process. How sad. Learning to master discipline is an investment of your time that will reap rich dividends. Please take time to pray about this and to become more diligent in your discipline.

On the spiritual level, when your teaching and discipline are dedicated to the honor of God, and you demonstrate the love of Christ and the dominance of the Holy Spirit in your teaching, discipline will come. On the mental level, when you have provided developmental foresight, defined your basic rules, decided on your system of cause and effect and discussed them with your students, discipline will come.

On the emotional level, when you deal with the details, stay detached from the things that don't matter, display humor, and don't yell, discipline will come. On the physical level, when you walk around the room frequently, use your eyes and hands to direct and redirect and discover the beauty in each child, discipline will come. One day you will discover that discipline has become second nature to you and teaching will be the blessing it was intended to be. Pray for discipline, and you will receive it. I do not believe that God intends for us to lose teachers over discipline. He will help you become the treasured teacher He wants you to be.

Treasured Teacher Training
As a dedicated teacher seeking to produce desirable discipline, what am I doing to:
- *demonstrate* the love of Christ?

_____

- allow the Holy Spirit *dominance* in my disciplining?

_____

- be *diligent* in my preparation?

_____

- *define* my basic rules?

_____

- *direct* my attention to the little things so they don't lead to the big things?

_____

- be willing to try new things as I discipline; such as being *dramatic*, singing, and playing fun games?

_____

- remember . . . *Don't yell.*

_____

- *deliver* my message with interest so I don't bore children, and create discipline problems?

_____

- *dignify* each child and *discover* positive and beautiful things in each of them?

_____

- *display* godly qualities to my students in my teaching?

_____

Methods and Materials

A Treasured Teacher teaches God's truth with excellence.

"Thy Word is a lamp to my feet, and a light to my path" (Psalm 119:105).

The teaching objective of this chapter is to demonstrate a variety of teaching methods that present God's Word with excellence.

Chapter Eight

I observed an excellent teacher give a group of four-year-olds a lesson about Creation. His teaching tools were in perfect order. He involved the children; they were completely mesmerized by the lesson. He moved his hand dramatically through the air as he asked, "And what did God create that is everywhere but not able to be seen?" One bright girl promptly responded, "Germs!" Hers was not exactly the answer he wanted, but it was definitely a correct answer. Our personal experience impacts learning. This child's family had recently battled frequent rounds of colds and flu, and I'm sure "germs" were very much a topic of conversation at their home. We may plan the greatest lesson in the world, but we must meet our learners where they are and begin from there.

A Treasured Teacher views each student as a special individual created by God for His perfect purpose. Each student is important to God and worthy of the most excellent teaching of His Word. We must be eager to try new ideas to reach students. In this chapter we will take a look at methods and materials to enrich your teaching.

If you are a new teacher, you may want to not read this chapter now. Use your teacher's manual and do the best you can to avoid "overload." Come back to this chapter later when you are ready to incorporate some new ideas. Be gentle and patient with yourself.

Guided Discovery Learning

Guided Discovery Learning as a Christian education principle links lives to biblical truths and leads learners to relate everything in life to Jesus Christ as Lord. It involves learners by helping pupils of all ages search out God's perspective on issues and needs. Guided Discovery Learning relates to life by exploring all of life's vital issues in light of God's Word.

Three steps in Guided Discovery Learning include:

- Focus: The teacher captures the pupils' attention and turns it toward the lesson's aim.
- Discover: Students discover and discuss what the Word of God says and begin to think of possible implications for their own lives.
- Respond: Pupils apply biblical truths to their lives and respond obediently to the Lord.

The goal of Christian education is not merely to produce people with unlimited knowledge of Bible facts, but people who are intellectually, spiritually, and emotionally transformed through a relationship with Jesus. Let's look at ways we can do this with each of our learners. We will give some suggestions by general age-groups (preschool and elementary). Most preschool children are still multisensory and respond well to any sensory teaching. At ages 7-9, children lean toward a more specific learning style.

Focus

LOOKER
Preschool:

- Pictures that illustrate a need or focus attention on the lesson
- Puzzles that focus attention on the lesson

Elementary:

- Maps that show where the Bible lesson occurred
- Time lines
- Flannelgraph to reenact/present/illustrate the lesson

TALKER
Preschool:

- Stories

- Puppets
- Music
- Drama
- Discussion

Elementary:
- Open-ended questions
- Problem to be solved
- Short tapes which focus attention on the lesson

TOUCHER
Preschool:
- Puzzles
- Blocks to build something related to the lesson

Elementary:
- Murals
- Felt lessons to do together

DOER
Preschool:
- Centers
- Blocks
- Puzzles
- Music with actions

Elementary:
- Drama
- Games
- Pantomime

FACT FINDER
Preschool:
- Light up boards
- Games

Elementary:
- Maps
- Time lines
- Bible games
- Sword drill

Please note: It is the responsibility of the teacher to guide the learning and participation at this level to gently FOCUS the child's attention toward the lesson aim. You will get better at this with practice.

Discover
This is the exciting part! We bring the child to God's Word where he can DISCOVER what God says about his need. Each learner will DISCOVER best when the lesson is presented in his own learning style.

LOOKER
Preschool:
- Pictures as you read to him from God's Word
- Felt board lessons
- Chalk talks (Draw something as you share from God's Word if you are artistically inclined)

Elementary:
- Bible reading
- Felt board lesson as you explore the lesson
- Visuals provided in your Resource packet

TALKER
Preschool:
- Listening as you read the passage with great voice inflection and excitement
- Discussion on the meaning of the passage
- Share experiences related to the lesson (You may guide with questions, such as, "Have you ever felt afraid? How do you think David felt when he went to fight Goliath? I wonder how he knew that God was on his side. Have you ever felt sure that God was with you at a time when you were afraid?")

Elementary:
- Reading the passage together
- Discussing what it means
- Sharing personal experiences
- Dialogues
- Debates on an issue

- Role play
- Drama

TOUCHER
Preschool:
- Clay to make something related to the lesson as you read it or share it as a story
- Puzzle related to the lesson
- Puppets to repeat the passage in their own words and understanding
- Anything they can touch that is related to the lesson and can be used as a teaching tool

Elementary:
- Finger-reading as you read from God's Word
- Mural relating the lesson to their own lives
- Puppets that articulate their understanding of what the passage means

DOER
Preschool:
- Puppets
- Drama
- Action-oriented songs (The best source for this is *Motions 'n Music* available from Scripture Press.)

Elementary:
- Raps written and performed by students. Raps can involve the whole body as they clap and rap.
- Role Play
- Musicals

FACT FINDER
Preschool:
- Presentation of as many facts as possible
- Objective background information about the passage
- "Life in Bible Times" historical background on the lesson

Elementary
- Same as above

- Time lines
- Maps

Respond

Now comes the critical time. We want the child to PERSON-ALLY RESPOND to the Bible lesson and begin to make a practical APPLICATION to his own life. Most teaching "misses the mark" here. We need the leading of the Holy Spirit and experience to know HOW to guide a child into a personal response and application of the lesson.

LOOKER
Preschool:

- Pictures of boys and girls from books and magazines that will lead them to a personal response. (If the lesson is on sharing, show pictures of children who are not sharing. Ask questions like: "Has this ever happened to you? When someone did not share with you, how did you feel? Have you ever not shared with someone? I think we might have all had a time when we didn't feel like sharing. Let's say WHY we didn't want to share." Then show pictures of children sharing and repeat a similar process.)
- Felt Board Lesson that leads to a personal response (As you show the lesson, stop and ask questions that make them think and reflect. "What would you do if this happened to you?" Let's pretend that we decided to . . . Now let's pretend that we did it God's way. How did it turn out differently? What can we do this week *to do it* God's way?)
- Dramatization of desirable and undesirable personal responses

Elementary:

- Open-ended pictures that students completed by drawing or writing out situations showing they did it the way they wanted, or did it God's way
- Notes that students write to themselves to help them to remember what to do in a particular situation (Use this as a time of helping them draw a personal conclusion and make an application to their life.)
- Charts to record their progress in an area and then share with the group next week

"Choose for yourselves today whom you will serve . . . but as for me and my house, we will serve the lord." *Joshua 24:15*

SUN.	MON.	TUES.	WED.	THURS.	FRI.	SAT.	TOTAL

☺___
☹___

If I forgot or failed to serve the Lord today, I will confess my sin and do better tomorrow. (Bring this chart back to class!)

TALKER
Preschool:
- Questions to guide sharing like, "What do you think this means? Has this ever happened to you?" If they aren't ready to *relate to it* yet, share examples from your own life or childhood. Children love this, and it gives them the freedom to be open and vulnerable also.
- Drama
- Role play, called "let's pretend" (For example, "Let's pretend that I am a new boy in our class. What are some things you can do to make me feel welcome?" Or, "How can you share Jesus with a friend on your street who is acting mean?")

Elementary:
- Guided discussion to encourage them to apply the truth of the lesson
- Role play
- Puppet shows that propose hypothetical situations (Children often reveal much more about their feelings with a pup-

128

pet in their hand behind a stage. Children third grade and above become very inhibited about expressing themselves in personal issues. However, they often will do it with a puppet. You must *verbalize it just right.* For example: "The preschool teacher asked if you could do a puppet show for their class about this lesson. Can you help them out?" Children are usually eager if they think they are "helping" or "teaching" younger children.)

TOUCHER
Preschool:
- Clay ("Let's show what might happen if we did things our own way ... now let's show what happened when the people in our lesson did it God's way.")
- Mural that shows two contrasting responses to a lesson
- Role play with puppets contrasting responses to the lesson.

Elementary:
- Murals related to application
- Shadow boxes that demonstrate an application of a Bible truth
- Role plays with hands (Pretend you are blind or deaf, and have them role play how they can apply the Bible lesson with their hands.)

FACT FINDER
Responding and applying a Bible lesson will be difficult for the Fact Finder because he wants things to be objectively stated. He wants black and white answers. Subjective discussions and self-reflection can be a challenge for him since they are outside of his comfort zone. He can recite all the facts of a lesson, and may even be able to tell you what is the "right" thing to do. But he may not be ready to see how this applies to him. Be patient with this learner during the RESPOND time and pray for the Lord to show you ways to reach him.

More methods and materials
Some games and activities to enhance your teaching are found in Appendix A and Appendix B. Addresses for other resources are listed in the Bibliography. Also, get in the habit

of looking to the Enrichment section of your teacher guide for a gold mine of additional activities.

Teaching with Centers

Teaching with centers can strengthen godly leadership qualities, particularly in energetic children. Centers give children many outlets for their abundant energy and teach godly character traits. Children learn patience ("wait for your turn in that center"), orderliness ("yes, you do have to clean it up before you can go on"), perseverance ("you do have to keep trying until you get it") and sharing ("yes, there are two people in the home center and we share").

Centers are Bible-based

Teaching with centers can be considered to be based on theological principles:

- God made each person as a unique individual
- God created us with a will
- God expects us to be responsible
- God created us for relationships with God and others[1]

Teaching with centers–101

What are Centers? Centers are a way of organizing curriculum so that the learner can choose from a variety of activities and move at his own pace. Centers are specifically designated areas of learning that focus on one aspect of the curriculum such as music, nature, science, or maps.

Why teach with Centers? Children are multisensory learners. Centers provide a wide variety of experiences in which the child uses his eyes, ears, and hands to learn. Centers support the "discovery" method of learning in which the child learns by interacting, and by his own experience he "teaches" himself.

Who are they for? All children can benefit from centers because they can be set up to meet the *individual* needs of the learner, and each child progresses at his own pace.

Where do I put them? Centers can be adapted to almost any space in your environment. (More on this later.)

When do I use them? Use Centers for *part* of the learning time. They are *one* of the ways that you teach.

How do I begin? Begin with a specific center and use it to teach the children about centers in general. Show them the center. Explain how to use it. Explain rules about using centers appropriately. As you achieve success, you can add more.

Learning centers
A learning center is:
1. a method of teaching;
2. a learning activity designed to accomplish specific objectives which can be done without continuous leader assistance;
3. a way of organizing tasks so that learners can make individual choices among a variety of activities and can work at their own pace;
4. a learning situation in which a number of learners may do several different assignments at the same time, choosing to work on one or more tasks appropriate to each individual's ability and interest level;
5. an activity, or several activities, designed to enable an individual or a group to accomplish a specific objective;
6. a way of organizing materials and tasks so that persons can make choices and direct their own learning.

Learning centers are a learning-through-play time with activities organized around a learning aim. Learning centers are various areas of your room where children may deal with the lesson material from one aspect or another. Sometimes learning centers help children become familiar with a particular Bible-time custom so they will better understand the Bible story. Other times learning centers emphasize an aim through looking at books, observing plants or animals, drawing a picture, or participating in creative play.

Learning centers are a change-of-pace from traditional Sunday School activities. They provide self-directed, independent learning experiences and allow the teacher to relate to each child as an individual. Preschoolers have many and varied needs. Learning centers divide the room and provide a familiar and comfortable setting. The most effective learning takes place one-on-one. Learning centers can be the best place to teach!

Eager-to-learn, active preschoolers need a bridge between

the thoughts and activities they left behind when they walked through the classroom door and the Bible story they are to hear. Activity centers provide that bridge by focusing the children's attention on the theme of the day or background for Bible truth. Truly, they are one way to "train up a child in the way he should go" (Prov. 22:6).

Preschoolers learn as they move and as they play. They learn through their senses: feeling, smelling, tasting, seeing, and hearing. We often neglect the first three!

If you share a room with another group, improvise as necessary. Boxes and piano benches have often served as learning center areas. As for the materials, use what you have available, following suggestions in these lessons. Make a systematic plan for acquiring supplies over a period of time.

Select the centers you will use in each lesson based on the number of children and their needs, the number of teachers, and space and equipment available. If you have only four children and one teacher, select one center idea and use that as a learning activity for the whole group.

Suggested centers vary from week to week to fit the aim of the lesson. You may wish to establish some centers permanently. For instance, the Home Living Center, Block Center, and the Art Center may always be in the same locations in your room.

Learning centers are basic to total-hour teaching. Children often begin coming in 10 minutes or so before Sunday School officially begins. Have the learning centers ready for them and make those early minutes count for God. If all your children arrive right on time, plan the first 10 or 15 minutes for learning center activities.

Here are a few more suggestions for using learning centers:

1. There should be a teacher or worker at each center to guide the children and lead discussions. But the teacher should make suggestions rather than dictate what the children are to do.
2. When centers are next to each other, folding dividers or bookcases may be used to help mark off the learning-center areas. If such are not available, you will find that most children operate successfully in a flexible situation.

Teachers are the ones who may find it hard to function with this flexibility! Just remember, they are good for the children.

3. Children may choose which center they wish to visit. When a child has completed an activity at one center, he or she may move to another.

4. Store materials for children to use and put them away on low, open shelves or in boxes on these shelves. Encourage children to develop the habit of putting things away when they are finished with them. (Keep inappropriate items on high shelves or out of sight.)

5. Do not display all possible materials every time a center is used. Put out only the items that pertain to the day's lesson or theme.

6. Use signals to conclude learning-center activity time. Give a warning signal several minutes ahead of time so children can begin putting things away and cleaning up. Then give the final signal to call the children to the next activity. (Use a pleasant-sounding bell, a chord on the piano, sing a song, or blink the lights.)

Learning centers require a little extra thought and planning, but the responses of the children make them well worth the effort. The functions of learning centers are to give children opportunities to manipulate objects which help develop perception and concepts, to develop problem-solving skills, to make choices and decisions, and to identify with other roles.[2]

Rules for using centers

1. We always put things back where we found them, and in proper order. Each item has a code that matches the code on the shelf. You must return items to the proper place and in proper order.

(I suggest coding each item with a dot that matches the dot on the shelf to help the child remember where to put it away.)

2. We use an inside (quiet) voice. If you are too loud, you will have to leave the center. I want to strongly encourage you to be very strict about this. Activity excites children and it can become loud or chaotic quickly. If you require only quiet, "inside" voices, it keeps the noise level very manageable.

3. Circulate continually to assist children, manage disci-

pline, and maintain order. Be a *pillar of peace* as you circulate. Whisper instructions, gently encourage, praise, pray, touch, affirm, and assist. You will be amazed at how much order your very presence can achieve.

4. Have the children review the rules before class begins. Invite the children one at a time to go to the centers. Invite them in a quiet voice. If it is getting too rowdy, ring the bell and quietly redirect or reverbalize the system.

**Attend to the details of order.
Little things do lead
to big things.**

Sample Centers

Preschool
Worship
Purpose: Provide an orderly area for children to be quiet and reflect on God's Word.
Procedure: Use a small table or shelf and add a pretty cloth, Bible, flowers. Show the children how quietly we can pray or read God's Word.
Presentation: Be reverent. Children are mimics. For little children, put picture Bibles and for Kindergarten to Grade 6 add Bibles that are age-appropriate for children. For example, for Kindergarten use a picture Bible such as:
- *My Picture Bible* by V. Gilbert Beers, Victor Books
- *The Bible for Little Eyes* by Kenneth Taylor
- *Read 'n' Grow Picture Bible,* Focus on the Family Edition, Sweet Publishers, Ft. Worth, Texas 76118
- *Illustrated Stories from the Bible,* Eagle Systems International, Community Press, Antioch, California 94509

Move to Bibles that have a third grade reading level, some pictures and reference keys to help the child. For example:
- *The Bible for Children* (Simplified Living Bible Text) Tyndale House Publishers Inc., Wheaton, Illinois
- *The Illustrated Bible,* David C. Cook, Elgin, Illinois
- *International Children's Bible,* Sweet Publishing, 1986, Ft. Worth, Texas, 76137

• *NIV Children's Bible,* Holy Bible, New International Version, Zondervan, 1978

Nature
Purpose: Encourage children to appreciate the incredible world God made and to help them feel a part of your class by bringing in "treasures" from home to share with the class.
Procedure: Let the children bring in their items. Let them discover and explore *carefully* on their own. This is an easy center to add because you don't have to do anything. The children do the work and assume ownership of the center.
Presentation: Be thankful to God for His wondrous creation. Treat each others' items with great care and respect.

Books
Purpose: Encourage children to love books and to read or look at books reinforcing the lesson.
Procedure: Put books related to the curriculum lesson in baskets or on shelves. Find nice big pillows or rocking chairs to make the book corner warm, cozy, and inviting. Show children how to open books, turn pages properly, and return them correctly.
Presentation: Be respectful and treat books with care and love. Books are our friends. Help children to fall in love with reading.

Art Center
Purpose: Provide different mediums for the child to express what he has learned from the lesson.
Procedure: Place a table, chair, and a variety of art mediums in the center for the child to create an art representation for the lesson. Add an easel if your budget and space allows.
Presentation: Be creative. Have open-ended projects in which a child can create his own interpretation and representation of the lesson. Have a structured art project, as well, with definitive steps to complete that project.

Bible Puzzles
Purpose: Allow the child to see, touch, and do Bible lesson puzzles.
Procedure: Provide a variety of age-appropriate puzzles on a

shelf or in a puzzle rack. Have puzzles that have a *knob* on each piece for preschoolers. This trains the pencil-grip reflex and is easier to manage for little fingers. Instructo-Judy has published large *floor* puzzles which are excellent for preschool because the pieces are big, durable, colorful, and easy to manage. Add jigsaw puzzles and move difficult puzzles for older children.

Presentation: Show the children how to do a puzzle correctly. Look at the picture to get it in our "mind's eye." Then take the pieces out carefully, put them "right side up" and put the picture together again.

Home and Family

Purpose: Allow young children to role-play real-life situations. Young children see work and play as synonymous. Valuable concepts like serving and sharing can be modeled and cultivated in this center.

Procedure: Use the character trait application of the lesson to help children play in a directed manner. This can be as simple or elaborate as your space and budget allows. It works as successfully with a box and some plastic dishes as with a complete play kitchen, living room, and bedroom. The key is *attitude.* Home living skills are what we are teaching.

Presentation: "Show me ways that we can *show* love to our family members." "What are ways that we can *serve* one another in our family?" "How many ways can we *give* to our family?" "What are some things that family members *share* with one another?" "How do we show *others* that we care by inviting them into our home?"

Listening

Purpose: Provide a place for children to learn through listening. This center is a special comfort zone for the auditory learner.

Procedure: Show the children the proper care of tapes, recorder, ear phones, and volume controls. If you can afford it, provide a tape recorder and tapes. Record players are not used as frequently these days, but certainly suffice. The "high tech" center of the '90s may include a CD player and CDs.

Presentation: "This is how we use our listening center. Here is where we find our tapes (records). This is how we turn the machine on. Here is a volume control." If you have ear phones, show them how we use them. If you don't, you may have to have rules for appropriate volume control. Show proper use and care of whatever you have put in the center.

Drama
Purpose: Most children love this center because they enjoy playing out situations. Little children love "make believe" and pretend.
Procedure: Simply have people bring in old clothes, hats, gloves, and purses. For a *Bible Drama Center,* simply save old bathrobes and towels. A *Puppet Center* can be elaborate or very simple. A table on its side or a cardboard box can serve as a puppet stage. They can be made with PVC pipe and curtains with a hem. Puppets can be made from bags or socks. Don't be limited in your thinking just because of limited resources.
Presentation: This center will get children more excited than others. You may have to limit it to two children at a time.

Elementary Centers:
The older children are, the more creative you have to be with centers. Children become more set in their particular learning styles and gravitate to the centers that specifically meet their learning needs. Keep changing or rotating the centers that you select so the learning is always fresh and able to meet the needs of the individual learner. Here are some suggestions. Remember, don't attempt all of them at one time. Change or rotate them.

Worship Center	Audiovisual Center
Book Center	Cooking Center
Art Center	Woodwork Center
Computer Center	Prayer Center
Bible Timeline Center	You Were There Center
Bible Maps Center	Game Center
Drama Center	Evangelism Center
Music Center	Missions Center
Listening Center	Puzzles Center
Parables Center	Creative Center

ABCs of Bible learning centers
To conclude, here are key points about centers.
Attitude is important in meeting students' needs.
Before you begin, think through the details.
Children can care for the centers if trained to do so.
Discipline is important to establish before you begin.
Evangelism is the part of your centers that counts for eternity.
Finishing what you begin is an important character trait to teach.
Godly character is our first priority.
How we introduce the center includes stating purpose and procedures.
Individual learning needs are best met with learning centers.
Jesus is to be lifted up in all we say and do.
Kindness should permeate the atmosphere.
Learning is multi-sensory for the young child.
Manners, please.
Nature centers are fun; children can bring in priceless treasures!
Open your mind, heart, and spirit to new ideas.
Parables can be "hands on" also.
Quiet voices help everyone learn more effectively.
Respect each other's work.
Space does not need to be a limitation.
Time-out chairs may be needed if a child chooses to disrupt.
Understand that things take time.
Verses can be memorized in the memory center.
With God, all things are possible.
(e)Xamine your attitude. Pray.
You can do it!
Zealously guard the rights of the individual learner.

Small-space Centers

If you have limited space, you can put hands-on items in a box and then set them out on the floor. For example, one teacher had to teach in the church kitchen, so we set up a box and arranged the items on the countertop in her "classroom." After class she boxed them up and took them home.

If you have space for only one shelf in your room, you can set up items on the shelf. The children can be invited one at a time to go to the shelf and select an item, take it to their place, complete it, and put it back.

Activities in a box or on a shelf
What kinds of items do we put on these shelves?

Puzzles with large pieces that go together on the floor are excellent for preschool; they involve shoulder action as well as hand-eye coordination. Instructo-Judy has excellent puzzles that teach Bible concepts, are bright and colorful, and child proof. Children can stomp on the pieces (no, we don't allow it but it could happen), and they won't break. For table top, try to get puzzles that have *knobs*. This trains the grip that teaches a child to hold a pencil correctly.

Clay can be used to teach almost any lesson. It is a wonderful item to have available for your kinesthetic learner. If you make your own, it will stay soft. Put it in an airtight container, and you will have it for a long time.

Play Dough Recipe

1 ½ c. flour
1 c. salt
1 t. powdered alum
1 t. vegetable oil
1 c. boiling water
food coloring

Mix dry ingredients. Add oil and water and stir vigorously with a wooden spoon. Add food coloring as desired and knead. This makes 2 cups of dough. Do not double this recipe for large amounts, but mix several recipes instead. For reusable play dough, store in a tightly covered container. This keeps several months. Objects made with these ingredients dry to a hard finish overnight. Put clay in a basket with cookie cutters and a small rolling pin and you have a complete center.

Books are always good for a child and most children love books. Put some books in a basket. Be sure to take time to teach children proper use and care of these valuable treasures.

God's Creations, or items that represent the seven days of Creation in a basket. The children can take them out and as they play you can encourage with verbalizations such as "God made the sun. God made the moon. God made the stars. God made the sun, moon, and stars on the fourth day."

An excellent source for these kind of items is Little Christian Supply, P.O. Box 1763, Blytheville, AR.

If you want to buy your own, go to a toy store and buy baby toys in the shape of the sun, moon, and stars. Get plastic farm or zoo animals for them to touch as well as taste. (Let's remember, little ones do put things in their mouth, so items can't be too little or children will choke.)

Bible Felt Board Betty Lukens puts out quiet felt books which teach six Bible lessons. You can get them for $10.00 each. Children love these. They are quiet and can keep children productive for a long time.

Elementary activities in a box or on a shelf
Bible Games (You can make them up or buy them in a Christian store.)
Bible Maps
Bible Parables
Bible Time lines
Bible Books
Art Mediums

The key is to keep changing the procedure of your teaching so that each child will eventually be taught in the way he learns best. Children don't say, "Oh, now she's teaching for those TALKERS, then we'll have to do centers for the TOUCHERS, but eventually she'll get back to teaching the "right" way for us LOOKERS. When you vary your teaching methods a rhythm comes that children learn to trust. They can't articulate *why* they feel relaxed and *why* they trust you to meet their individual needs, they just do.

Ideas for Enhancing Children's Church

The Children's Church hour is often a time when we can try new teaching ideas. Scripture Press publishes a Children's Church Curriculum which works well for this hour. Some Children's Church programs sometimes run longer than an hour, and additional activities may be needed. Use centers to generate additional activities. You may consider some of the following ideas.

Although we need to vary our teaching for individual learning needs, we need to vary how we teach entire classes.

When you teach large groups of children, creativity in the presentation is very important.

Puppets
I am convinced that you can teach most anything with a puppet because children love puppets! An adult can be tuned out by many children. But when a puppet says the exact same words, children listen! Take advantage of this fact to enhance your teaching.

A longstanding rule of mine is that when someone is talking (who has permission), we are quiet and listen. When we do puppet shows, I say, "If we are loud and not listening, our puppets friends will be sad and go away." If the children are loud, the puppets are lowered. If the children become quiet, the puppets return. If the children continue to talk, the puppets do not come back. An adult can explain, "Our puppet friends have so many wonderful things to share with you, but they could not be heard. They told me that they want to come back, and they hope you will remember to be very quiet."

In twenty years of using puppets, I find that you only need to take the puppets away once, and you will have "good listeners" from there with that group of children.

Storyboard
This may be a new concept for your school or church. My dear friend, Claude Edge, built one for me and I have used it for hundreds of lessons. In fact, when Christmas fell on a Sunday, the senior pastor asked me to use it in "big church." During the first service, he observed from the front of the church. He said that he had never seen adults so attentive. During the next service he joined the audience. Mr. Storyboard is now a regular part of the Family Time at the evening service, and used for special events.

To build a storyboard, begin with a wooden frame, like a window frame with glass or plexiglass in it. It can be any size, depending upon how many people will need to see it. Ours has been used for up to 500 people. The framed glass should be placed on rolling legs so it can be easily moved. Put fluorescent lights across the top of the back of the frame, and put a skirt around the bottom of the board so you will not be able to tell someone is behind the board.

SPECIAL MINISTRIES

Mr. Story Board:

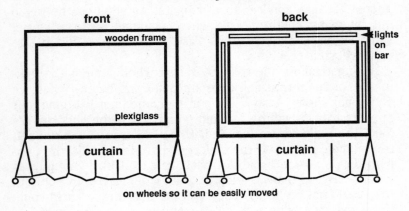

front   back

wooden frame   lights on bar

plexiglass

curtain   curtain

on wheels so it can be easily moved

With the lights of the storyboard on, a person who is *behind* the board uses thick colored markers to draw over a light pencil drawing on white butcher paper fitted and taped to the framed glass.

In front of the storyboard, another person teaches the lesson which corresponds to the drawing. The lights prevent the children from seeing anything other than the drawings appearing on the board.

See Appendix A for more creative ideas for use with an entire group.

Music As a Tool to Teach the Bible

I believe music is one of the best ways to teach concepts. If a person can sing something, he will remember it. Children can learn anything faster when it's put to music. How can we use music in our teaching?

Teaching hymns of the faith

Teaching children the hymns of the faith is a very important part of our heritage. Children don't always learn hymns as quickly as they do other songs. They may balk initially because hymns aren't as easy to learn as other songs. A great way to begin is to use the Psalty Seven tape which is a "Travel through Time to Great Hymn Writers." It makes hymns "come alive" for children, and they love it.

I believe children can learn one hymn a month. Your particular church or school may have their favorites. In case they don't, here's a suggested listed for your first year.

January:	It Is Well with My Soul
February:	God Bless America
March:	Christ the Lord Is Risen Today
	I Am the Resurrection
April:	I'll Go Where You Want Me to Go
May:	Savior Like a Shepherd
June:	Oh, How I Love Jesus
July:	When the Roll Is Called up Yonder
August:	Stand Up for Jesus
September:	Trust and Obey
October:	Holy, Holy, Holy
November:	This Is My Father's World
December:	Christmas Carols

Contemporary music

There is so much contemporary Christian music on the market today. It is a real challenge to keep up with what is available. Here are a *few* of the many I use.

1. Children love all the Psalty tapes. Here's the theme of some of the many available.

Psalty Six:	Heart to Change the World (Missions)
Psalty Seven:	Hymn Writers
Psalty Eight:	Play Ball!
Psalty Ten:	Salvation Celebration

2. The Donut Man has excellent tapes which teach Bible lessons and character trait application.

There are tapes that teach academic subjects such as math, states and capitals, and phonetic sounds. These can make a significant difference as to whether or not the auditory learner can learn these subjects.

143

Scripture verses to music
One of the most effective ways to teach memory verses is to put them to music. An added dimension is to also teach sign language. You don't need to be trained in signing to do this: you can simply add some motions that help the child to remember the words. If you are blessed to have someone in your school or church who does sign, it can be a great way to teach the verses. For example:

1. Sing the verse with the children.
2. Then say it and sign it.
3. Then sign it in silence.
4. Then sing and sign.

You can vary the process. The children will have a much higher level of retention.

Lessons to music
There are excellent resources on the market today that teach lessons to music. Check your local teacher supply store, Christian bookstore, or secular bookstore. I have listed a few in the Resource Section, but there are many more!

Music fun and movement
Little children need to move. Most elementary age children love to move, but are more self-conscious. Take the time to learn some age-appropriate songs that involve action and movement. On those days when nothing is working (and we all have them!) do some action songs. They will be a positive way to get the "wiggles" out and help students concentrate on the lesson later. The songbook and tapes *Motions 'n Music* from Scripture Press are excellent for this.

Music cues
If you play the piano and if you have a piano in your classroom, this is an effective way to communicate simple instructions to the children. You can say, "Did you hear what Mr. Piano told you to do?" Like puppets, the piano depersonalizes the "lecturing" and makes the lesson more fun for the children. These ideas are from the book by Brenda Taylor, 2014 Willingham Drive, Richardson, Texas 75080.

Character traits
Character traits such as honesty, kindness, and joy are important concepts to teach, even if you don't teach in a Christian organization.

Put them into songs with a fun beat; children love learning about them. It will do your heart good when you hear a child humming, or singing the song as he plays outside. Messages stay with children so much longer when put to music.

Teaching Bible Memory

Most Bible curriculums provide their own Bible memory program. Sometimes children get one verse to learn on Sunday morning, another one for their Wednesday night club program, and still another for their school. Many children are put in "overload," and they can't master any of it. It is better for children to master a few verses, instead of having a general knowledge of many. I developed a Bible Memory Program for our school and church. It is too long to list here completely, but to summarize:

Age 2:	Twelve short verses-one per month
Age 3:	ABCs of Bible Memory from ACSI
Age 4:	ABCs of Bible Memory from Level One, Bible Memory Association
Kindergarten:	ABCs of Proverbs, Lord's Prayer
Grade One:	Books of the Bible, Ten Commandments
Grade Two:	Verses from the Fruits of the Spirit. (For example, in September two to four verses on Love, in October on Joy, November on Peace, etc.)
Grade Three:	Large passages and verses from Psalms
Grade Four:	Verses on Sharing the Gospel (see chapter 12) and the Beatitudes
Grade Five:	Verses and passages from the Book of John
Grade Six:	Guidelines on Holy Living from Galatians, Ephesians, Colossians, and Philippians

You can develop a program for your church or school, based on the priorities you have.

The "Well Versed Kids" Bible Memory program published

by NavPress is well organized and covers issues in which kids need to be grounded. There is an excellent guide to teach the meaning and application of each verse.

Another Bible memory program that can be adapted to any organization is BMA. It is individualized and provides wonderful incentives such as books and attending their summer camp. (See Resource section for addresses.)

Regardless of the system you select or develop, the key is: "Get children memorizing God's Word!" In these times of increasing worldly temptations, we need to protect our children with proper spiritual attire.

What an adventure teaching is. The exciting part is that you learn more than your students. Anytime I have wanted to learn more about something, I try to teach it to someone. As I research the subject, I grow. But the real learning occurs when I GIVE it to someone else. I think this is why it is truly more blessed to give than to receive.

In writing this book, I realized that there are many more books I need to write. There are many more methods and materials to share. The longer I teach, the more I realize how very little I know. But that is what keeps me going. I love the process. I love teaching. I love learning. I pray that this book will be a friend that will stay with you for many years as you learn, grow, have a desire to stretch, and try new things.

Leading a Child to Christ

A Treasured Teacher knows that leading a child to Christ and helping him to grow in Jesus Christ is the most important work that he will ever do.

"Go therefore and make disciples of all the nations, baptizing them in the name of the Father and the Son and the Holy Spirit, teaching them to observe all that I commanded you; and lo, I am with you always, even to the end of the age" (Matthew 28:19-20).

The teaching objective of this chapter is to convict the teacher of the importance of presenting the Gospel and to present practical ways to share Christ and help students grow in Jesus.

Chapter Nine

Some dear friends have two very spiritually mature daughters, but their third child doesn't seem to be taking things quite so seriously. Even though she is only three, the two big sisters have been really working on her. Laura and Anna Grace asked Alyssa, "Do you know how you can get to heaven?"

She promptly replied, "Sure!"

"How?"

"On an airplane!"

To help her begin to reflect more deeply about her possible spiritual plight, they asked with great dismay, "Alyssa, do you want to go where there is fire all the time. What would you do there?"

Alyssa, not to be dismayed, replied, "I would just roast marshmallows!"

I don't think we have to worry about Alyssa's future. She is being raised in a strong, Christian home with very godly parents. However, we do need to worry about the world in general. We must put the issue of salvation at the top of our teaching priorities if we are to teach with an eternal focus.

Understanding Salvation

Leading others to Jesus Christ lies at the core of this book. A TREASURED TEACHER TRANSFORMS LIVES FOR JESUS CHRIST. All the other teaching we do remains at the periphery if the student is not transformed by the saving knowledge of Christ and changed from the **inside out.**

I was one of those people who thought if I went to church and was a "good" person, I would, of course, go to heaven. I was an adult when I clearly understood the Gospel and received Jesus Christ as my personal Savior. Then my life began to be transformed. My hunger for the Word and to know Jesus did not begin until I was born again. Before that time, I was very works-oriented.

My personal experience has made me especially committed to children knowing Scripture, hearing the Gospel, and understanding what it means to be "born again." Since children are literal learners, the concept of "born again" can be approached from many angles. This shows us how dependent we are on the Holy Spirit to help us teach God's message to a child.

The lesson on Nicodemus and being born again can pose a teaching challenge. I had every angle covered (or so I thought!) to ensure my class's understanding. "Did this mean that Nicodemus came out of his mommy's tummy again?" "What does it mean to be born of the spirit?" That night a parent called to tell me her daughter accepted Christ with her father. They were thrilled because she had been able to clearly articulate her decision, and they believed she truly was born again. However, when bedtime came, she began to cry. "Since I am born again, do I have to sleep in my crib again?" Back to the drawing board.

Because I am aware of the danger of teaching that is not connected to a personal relationship with Jesus Christ, I constantly ask children questions, such as:

● "I guess you will be going to heaven since you are coming to Sunday School, right?" (No! Why?)

● "Think of a time that you were really, really good. Now do you think Jesus would let you go to heaven *because of how* good you were that day?" (No! Why?)

● "I am praying for each of you to know Jesus and to be able to go to heaven. Will this get you to heaven? How about if your mommy and daddy pray this for you? (No! Why?)

Finally, the most important question: "If Jesus came back through the clouds today, would He take you with Him to heaven?" (Why? Why not?)

Continually provide checks like these to be sure your students understand that salvation is a personal decision that no one can make for them. They must KNOW that they are a sinner, and INVITE Jesus Christ to be their Lord and Savior on their very own. Often a child wants Jesus, but may not yet be convicted of his sin nature.

Coming to grips with our sin nature is a prerequisite to the Christian life. Sometimes a child will be able to tell you all the "bad" things that his friends or other family members did (often revealing more of what HE did), but he will look you right in the eye and tell you that he doesn't do any of those bad things. A child may think that since he hasn't committed the "big (time) sins" such as killing, he really isn't a sinner.

A child needs to discern the difference between being sorry he got caught and being sorry he sinned. I use many stories and analogies to help children deal with this major issue. When we realize that Romans 3:23 which says "ALL have sinned and fall short of the glory of God" really means EACH of us, then the process has begun.

The next hurdle is then learning to deal with the sin inside of us by confessing it and asking forgiveness. To illustrate this for children, take a bar of soap and on the soap wrapping write, "If we confess our sins, He is faithful and righteous to forgive us our sins and to cleanse us from all unrighteousness" (1 John 1:9). I thank my friend, Sue Bohlin, for sharing this idea. It serves as a practical reminder that just as we need to wash our bodies each day, we must confess our sins each day to stay spiritually clean.

Tools for Sharing the Gospel
There are many helpful tools available to help you present the Gospel. Strong evangelical Sunday School curriculums such as those developed by Scripture Press *weave this* into their lesson. There are also many other organizations that have published materials on this as well:

● Child Evangelism Fellowship (*The Gospel Glove* and *The Wordless Book*)

- Evangelism Explosion
- NavPress
- Association of Christian Schools International

Statistics tell us that 85 percent of the people who come to a saving knowledge of Jesus Christ do so BEFORE the age of eighteen, and 62 percent before the age of twelve. Is there any stronger motivation for mastering this skill as part of your teaching ministry?

So where can we begin when we are new at sharing the Gospel with children?

Sharing our testimony
This is often one of the best ways to share the Gospel because
- We already know it. It is our personal experience, and we probably won't forget it, even if we are a little nervous.
- Sharing how we became CONVICTED of our sin and our need of a Savior prompts a similar response in others because of the authenticity of our story.
- We can mark key verses in our Bible that may be *guiding lights* for another.

Key verses in explaining salvation to children
Study the key verses below. Find the ones you are comfortable with and mark them in your own Bible with a highlighter, bookmark, or ribbon.

1. Each child must be aware he has need of a Savior because of his sinful nature:
   - Romans 3:10 "There is none righteous, not even one."
   - Romans 3:23 "For all have sinned and fall short of the glory of God."
   - Romans 6:23 "For the wages of sin is death, but the free gift of God is eternal life in Christ Jesus our Lord."
   - John 3:16-18 "For God so loved the world, that He gave His only begotten Son, that whoever believes in Him shall not perish, but have eternal life. For God did not send the Son into the world to judge the world, but that the world should be saved through Him.

He who believes in Him is not judged; he who does not believe has been judged already, because he has not believed in the name of the only begotten Son of God."

- 1 John 5:12-13 "He who has the Son has the life; he who does not have the Son of God does not have the life."
- John 5:24 "Truly, truly, I say to you, he who hears My word, and believes Him who sent Me, has eternal life, and does not come into judgment, but has passed out of death into life."
- Isaiah 12:2 "Behold God is my salvation; I will trust and not be afraid: For the Lord God is my strength and song, And He has become my salvation."

2. We want the child to know that God loves him very much:
- John 3:16 "For God so loved the world, that He gave His only begotten Son, that whoever believes in Him should not perish, but have eternal life."
- Luke 19:10 "For the Son of Man has come to seek and to save that which was lost."
- Ephesians 2:8 "For by grace you have been saved through faith; and that not of yourselves, it is the gift of God."

3. The child needs to understand that Jesus took the punishment for his sin:
- 1 Peter 2:24 "He himself bore our sins in His body on the cross, that we might die to sin and live to righteousness; for by His wounds you were healed."
- Revelation 1:5b "To Him who loves us, and released us from our sins by His blood."
- 1 Peter 3:18 "For Christ also died for sins once for all, the just for the unjust, in order that He might bring us to God, having been put to death in the flesh, but made alive in the spirit."

151

A Gospel acrostic (from Child Evangelism Fellowship)

G God is love	John 3:16	"For God so loved the world, that He gave His only begotten Son, that whoever believes in Him should not perish, but have eternal life."
O Only perfect Son	Galatians 4:4	"But when the fulness of time came, God sent forth His Son, born of a woman, born under the Law."
S Sin	Romans 3:23	"For all have sinned and fall short of the glory of God."
P Precious Blood	Revelation 1:5b	"To Him who loves us, and released us from our sins by His blood."
E Ever-lasting	Acts 16:31	"And they said, 'Believe in the Lord Jesus, and you shall be saved, you and your household."
L Let Jesus be your Savior	Ephesians 2:8-9	"For by grace you have been saved through faith; and that not of yourselves, it is the gift of God; not as a result of works, that no one should boast."

A shortened version
- *Bad News:*
  1. You are a sinner (Romans 3:23).
  2. The penalty for sin is death (Romans 6:23).
- *Good News:*
  1. Christ died for you (Romans 5:8).
  2. You can be saved through faith (Ephesians 2:8-9).
  3. Jesus is Lord (Romans 10:9).
- *Assurance:* John 5:24

Other Resources for Sharing the Gospel
Many different tools provide instruction on how to present the Gospel. Your church may have a particular set of materi-

als that they prefer you use in presenting the Gospel.

Larry Moyer has written some excellent material on presenting the Gospel. The address to write for these publications is in the Resource Section.

Acorn Publications has developed a children's curriculum called "Go Ye into All the Block." It uses the same verses, principles, and color-coding used by Child Evangelism Fellowship and gives six weeks of crafts which reinforce the Gospel message. Our church used it for a six-week Missions unit; the children responded very positively, and they were able to articulate the Gospel with great clarity. It was a good way for the unsaved children to hear the Gospel and gave the saved child some tools to articulate the Gospel and share with others. The address for Acorn Publications is in the Resource Section as well.

Tracts can be purchased very inexpensively in any Christian store. They have special ones for each holiday as well. The Gospel message remains the same, but there are different ways to express it. Find the verses, words, and stories that make the Gospel message the most clear for you and that will help you be more confident as you share the message. There is no more beautiful experience than being able to lead a child to Christ. When you see a young child be able to verbalize what it means to be washed in the blood of Jesus, you will stand in awe of the Spirit of God Who can give spiritual discernment, even to little ones.

**We FOCUS the child to show him
his need of a Savior because of
his sin nature. We guide him to
God's Word to DISCOVER God's
plan for him. We lead him to a
personal RESPONSE of praying
to accept Christ as his Lord
and Savior.**

Sharing the Gospel with Specific Learners

Children learn in different ways and are multi-sensory learners. I have experienced excellent results with the Child

Evangelism Fellowship and Acorn material because they provide opportunities for young children to use all of their senses as they learn about the Gospel. Let us look at ways we have to vary our approach to reach individual learners:

LOOKER:
He wants to SEE things, and so we
- show him key verses in the Bible
- show him the Wordless book

TALKER:
He wants to HEAR AND TALK about things, so we
- share our testimony with him
- let him talk about times he has *"goofed up"* in his life
- read the passages aloud to him with great voice inflection and let him discuss what they mean

TOUCHER:
This child needs to TOUCH something to best learn, so we
- provide him with materials published by Child Evangelism, such as the Wordless Book and the Gospel Glove
- let him look up the passages in his own Bible or follow along with his finger as you read

DOER:
This child wants to DO something as he is learning, so we
- provide Child Evangelism materials
- sing *Songs with Actions* related to the Gospel
- make crafts from the Acorn curriculum

FACT FINDER: This child wants the FACTS, so we
- give him the straight Gospel message
- show him verses that verify the messages in the Scriptures
- give him something that explains the Gospels in a sequential and analytical way, such as some of the drawings from NavPress

The Time to Begin Is Now
If giving the Gospel message is a new experience, begin TODAY to prepare yourself for this most important mission.

As you prepare, you will grow tremendously yourself. Remember, different techniques work for different people. Some may want to look up verses and write them out. Others may want to discuss the Gospel message with a friend first in order to get comfortable and internalize your plan. Still others simply need to DO it. Do what you need to do, but do it now.

Taking a stand

I had the opportunity of hearing Dr. Dobson and Gary Bauer discuss their book, *Children at Risk*. They say there is a civil war raging in the United States over the hearts and minds of our children. I agree completely.

As a teacher in the nineties, our job is more important than ever. Not only are we battling the overt influences of evil such as drugs, sex, and violence, we are battling insidious evils, such as the New Age Movement and humanism. We must take a stand, regardless of where we teach or what we teach.

Shifting trends

In the fifties we saw emphasized the inherent Judeo-Christian values of honesty, integrity, and the Protestant work ethic (working hard to earn a living). Values began to shift dramatically in the sixties. In the seventies, values that were perpetrated were more superficial, such as "winning by intimidation." The eighties brought us instant everything from the *One Minute Manager* to "Minute Mothering." What are we embracing in the nineties?

As Dr. Dobson and Gary Bauer contrasted the sixties and the nineties, they could have been describing separate centuries. We have become desensitized to the changes around us. Adults can remember the fifties and sixties. But what about our children?

Children need us more than ever before to take a stand on issues such as drugs, sex, abortion, and homosexuality. They are being raised in a world that presents these sins as the "norm." The world's values bombard them from everywhere: television, billboards, movies, books, and textbooks. What we see repeatedly is what we begin to integrate as reality. What are our children perceiving as the "norm"?

Dobson and Bauer stated, "The hottest battle is over the

rights of children and how they will be taught. The primary strategy is to drive a wedge between parents and children." They used the expression "corridors of childhood." Who is there to guide our children as they walk the ever increasing challenging "corridors of childhood?"

It is you, the teacher. Don't count on parents always being there for a child; they may not be. We must be there for the children. Let's be that Treasured Teacher, the one who educates for eternity, permeates the periphery and leads the child to Christ. Let's begin to transform lives *today* for Jesus Christ. Let's make a difference. Let's do it today.

But the goal of our instruction
is love from a pure heart and
a good conscience
and a sincere faith (1 Tim. 1:5).

Appendix A

Here are some prayer projects you might enjoy trying with your students. We can never overemphasize the power of prayer.

Prayer Time Lines

My son's third grade teacher, Leslie Kreatschman, had a very effective way of integrating prayer and current events. She placed a large time line on the wall. The children brought in items from the newspaper. They place them strategically on their time line and prayed about them. The Persian Gulf War was being waged, and it was exciting for the children to see the power of prayer at work.

Prayer Journals

Prayer journals can teach children to observe how God answers prayer. Have the children keep a spiral notebook with a page for each student. Each time they pray, they write a request for a particular child. When the prayer is answered, they jot a note about the result! This builds several good habits:
- Praying for others
- Seeing how God works to answer prayer
- Training to look for God's blessings in unexpected ways

Prayer Card Files

Prayer card files teach prayer techniques as well as organization. Give each student a card file box and a set of twenty-six tabs. Each students labels his tabs (i.e., classmates, teachers, his school, his church, family members, his country and its leadership, his state and its leadership, his city and its leadership, missionaries.

Each day the student writes down his prayer request on a 3 x 5 note card. When he is done praying for the requests, he files them under the appropriate tab. Once a week he goes through his cards and if a request has been answered, he writes the answer on the back of the card and files it under a tab called "Answers to Prayer."

Prayer Acrostic
Do a prayer acrostic as a class project on a poster and leave in the room, or each student may make his own. For example:

Personal renewal
Reveal sin in me
Ask and it will be given to me.
Yes, Lord. Use me.
Evangelism
Righteousness

Prayer Book Marks
Strips of card stock or poster board can be cut to the size of bookmarks. Have each student write their favorite prayer verse on their bookmark. They can decorate the front with markers or stickers. Encourage them to keep the bookmark in their Bibles.

Prayer Stand Up Cards
Cut card stock in 4" x 10" length. Have the students write the names of each classmate on the front of the card. Then bend it in half so it will stand up. Students can take the cards home, and then stand the card somewhere in their rooms where they will see it often. The card is a reminder to pray for their classmates during the week.

Prayer Testimonies
Students love to hear how God has answered prayers. Not only is it a positive testimony for students, it trains them to discern how God works and to recognize the blessings, even if God didn't answer the way they wanted.

Dramas on the Privilege
Once I felt the older children at our school (grades 6-9) were in a dry spell about prayer, I had a few fathers dress up as soldiers with pretend guns. In the middle of prayer time, they burst into the room and yelled, "You're right, they are praying. Line them up. They're going to jail."

Needless to say, this got the students' attention. We had studied about countries where people were not free to worship and pray, but the message had not hit home. Since then, the children took their prayer life more seriously. It is a privilege to talk to our Heavenly Father.

Appendix B

Time Machine

Purpose:
The purpose of the Time Machine is to acquaint children personally with Bible characters and heroes.

Procedure:
The Time Machine can be any of the following:
1. *A simple door* through which a person walks.
2. A painted *refrigerator box* with lights and decorations. The person who is to be the one interviewed comes out through the box OR the children can crawl through the box to be "transported" to another time.
3. My very creative friend, Fred Hennighausen, designed and built an elaborate time machine for me. We needed a simple machine for our VBS to "bring in" the missionaries we were studying: Amy Carmichael and Hudson Taylor. I discovered that the word *simple* is not in this man's vocabulary.

The "Time Machine" Fred designed was a plywood box on wheels, large enough to hold a small adult in *one-half* of the interior. The interior of the box was divided into two sections by a panel on hinges that could be opened to allow the person hiding in one half of the box access to the other half, from which he would emerge as the character.

Before the presentation, the character is hidden in the closed half of the box. From there, he will cause the special effects that are used to create the illusion of a working "machine." To add "authenticity," the time machine "operator" dons safety goggles, a hard hat plugged into the machine by a phone cord, and safety gloves. It's a good idea to explain to the children that time machines are quite tricky, and it's impossible to tell what might happen. This will "cover" any miscues between the operator and the hidden actor. It is also essential to open up the door of the machine at some point early in the presentation so that children see the "empty" machine.

The exterior of this machine was covered with plasticized mirrors and various lights, switches, and wires.

To begin, the machine must be turned on. One of the fake switches on the front is flipped while the actor flips the real switch on the inside, turning on twinkling Christmas lights placed across the front of the machine.

Various other lights, switches, and dials were added to give the illusion of choosing a time period and programming the computer. (This machine had a leaf blower inside to make loud noise when it was transporting people.) Use your imagination! The more "stuff" the better!

Presentation:
There is a "catch-22!" We want to make the presentation very real and the person authentic. However, we must clearly explain that we are not "beaming people down" from heaven. We are using this as a tool and not as a New Age mind trick. Always close with an explanation: "Children, it was interesting to have Amy Carmichael here so we could ask her questions about her life as a missionary. What did we learn about Amy Carmichael? (Allow for sharing.) Children, was it *really* Amy Carmichael? No, the *real* Amy Carmichael died and because she believed in Jesus, where is she now? Yes, in heaven. This was a person *pretending* to be Amy Carmichael to help us understand her life." As much fun as it is to pretend, we must be sure to state the truth. Children love this teaching tool.

Wheel of Scripture

Purpose:
The purpose of the Wheel of Scripture is to teach groups Scripture verses and to promote Bible Memory.

Procedure:
1. Make a wheel on particle board. Attach it to a pole with a mounting that will allow it to spin freely.
2. Make a frame that will house the letters. Put coffee cup hooks on the frame to hold the letters.

WHEEL OF SCRIPTURE

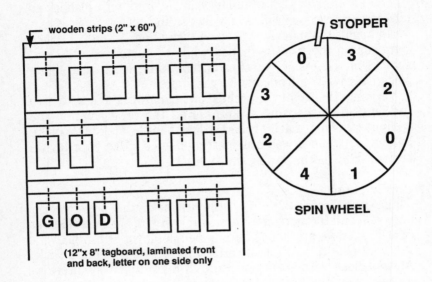

wooden strips (2" x 60")

STOPPER

SPIN WHEEL

(12"x 8" tagboard, laminated front and back, letter on one side only

3. Cut out poster board rectangles, 12" × 8". Write the letters on the board with a thick marker. Holepunch the top so it will go on the coffee cup hook.

Presentation:
Put a verse on the board with the letters facing the wall. Divide the group into two teams. Have a representative from each side spin the wheel, which has been marked with numbers. From this point, the game is played much like the "Wheel of Fortune" TV game show. If the spin lands on a number other than zero, the team guesses a letter in the verse. If they guess a letter in the verse, they get another turn. If the letter is not in the verse, the other team spins. If a spin lands on a zero, that team loses its turn. The first team to guess the Scripture correctly "wins." A bonus is given for the reference.

Drama

Purpose:
The purpose of drama is to bring life to Bible lessons.

Procedure:
Have a basket of "costumes" consisting of donated bath robes and towels for Bible dramas and other clothing for other dramatizations.

Presentation:
Read the Bible lesson or play a tape of the lesson. An excellent source for preschool stories is: Bible Stories for Little Ears by Perfect Sound Productions, Inc., Wheaton, Illinois.

An excellent source for elementary ages is: *You Are There,* also by Perfect Sound Productions. A wonderful book and tape is *Motions 'n Music* (Scripture Press) which takes Bible lessons and puts them to music as well as motions. Children 3-7 love these.

Discuss the lesson and how you will dramatize it.

Decide what each child will do as you dramatize it.

Another resource that will add an exciting dimension to your "hands-on" learning materials is Mike Bolinsky. One of my favorites is a twenty-foot whale that will allow you to conduct a class with twenty-five children sitting INSIDE the whale. He also has a special urn which can be used for teaching the lesson of Elisha and the widow. Contact Mike at Box 833, Cedar Hill, Texas 75104.

Notes

Chapter One: Transformed Teachers
[1]Benjamin R. DeJong, *Uncle Ben's Quotebook* (Eugene, Oregon: Harvest House Publishers, 1976), p. 70
[2]R.G. Delnay, *Teach As He Taught: How to Apply Jesus' Teaching Methods* (Chicago: Moody Press, 1987), p. 19.
[3]Edward Kuhlman, *Master Teacher* (Old Tappan, New Jersey: Fleming H. Revell, Co., 1987), p. 75.
[4]C. Peter Wagner, *Your Spiritual Gifts Can Help Your Church Grow* (Glendale, California: Regal Books, 1979), p. 122.
[5]Leslie Flynn, *Nineteen Gifts of the Spirit* (Wheaton, Illinois: Victor Books, 1974), p. 74.
[6]Ibid., p. 75.

Chapter Three: How to Put Together a Lesson
[1]Scripture Press Lesson, Unit 2, Lesson 7, p. 49, October 13, 1991, p. 49.

Chapter Four: Powerful Praying
[1]Richard J. Foster, *Celebration of Discipline* (San Francisco: Harper and Row, 1978), p. 33.
[2]E.M. Bounds, *Power Through Prayer* (Chicago: Moody Press, n.d.) p. 23.
[3]Ibid., p. 38.
[4]Benjamin R. DeJong, *Uncle Ben's Quotebook* (Eugene, Oregon: Harvest House, 1976), p. 250.
[5]Charles Stanley, *Handle with Prayer* (Wheaton, Illinois: Victor Books, 1982), p. 95.
[6]James J. Metcalf, *Teacher's Treasury* (Pasadena, California: National Educators Fellowship, 1980).

Chapter Five: Need for Nurturing
[1]Kenneth O. Gangel and Howard G. Hendricks, editors, *The Christian Educator's Handbook on Teaching* (Wheaton, Illinois: Victor Books, 1988), p. 13.

Notes

[2]Lois E. LeBar, *Education That is Christian* (Old Tappan, New Jersey: Fleming H. Revell Co.), p. 51.
[3]Benjamin R. DeJong, *Uncle Ben's Quotebook* (Eugene, Oregon: Harvest House Publishers, 1976), p. 59.
[4]Dr. James Plueddemann, *Education That Is Christian*, (Wheaton, Illinois: Victor Books, 1989), p. 150.
[5]Joe Temple, *Know Your Child* (Grand Rapids: Baker Books House, 1974), p. 31.

Chapter Six: Caring Communication
[1]Eleanor Doan, *Speaker's Sourcebook* (Grand Rapids: Zondervan, 1968), p. 66.
[2]Benjamin R. DeJong, *Uncle Ben's Quotebook* (Eugene, Oregon: Harvest House Publishers, 1976), p. 8.
[3]Howard Hendricks, *Teaching to Change Lives* (Portland: Multnomah Press, 1987), p. 84.

Chapter Seven: Desirable Discipline
[1]Benjamin R. DeJong, *Uncle Ben's Quotebook* (Eugene, Oregon: Harvest House Publishers, 1976), p. 131.
[2]Ibid., p. 140.

Chapter Eight: Methods and Materials
[1]Rachel Gillespie Lee, *Learning Centers for Better Christian Education* (Valley Forge, Judson Press, 1982).
[2]Scripture Press Curriculum, used by permission.

General Bibliography

Bolton, Barbara, Wesley Haystead and Charles T. Smith. *Everything You Want to Know about Teaching Children.* Ventura, California: Regal Books, 1987.

Ciona, John R. *Solving Church Education's Ten Toughest Problems.* Wheaton, Illinois: Victor Books, 1990.

Coleman, Robert E. *The Master Plan of Discipleship,* Old Tappan, New Jersey: Fleming H. Revell Co., 1987.

Costa, A.L. (Ed.) *Developing Minds: A Resource Book for Teaching Thinking.* Alexandria, Virginia: Association for Supervision and Curriculum Development, 1985.

Covey, Stephen R. *Principle-Centered Leadership.* New York, New York: Summit Books, 1991.

Crabb, Lawrence J., Jr. *Understanding People.* Grand Rapids, Michigan: Zondervan, 1987.

Dobson, Dr. James and Gary Bauer. *Children at Risk.* Waco, Texas: Word, 1990.

Elkind, David. *Miseducation: Preschoolers at Risk.* Alfred A. Knopf, 1987.

Fine, Eddie and Billye Joyce. *Teachers Are Made, Not Born.* Cincinnati, Ohio: Standard Publishing, 1990.

Flynn, Leslie. *Nineteen Gifts of the Spirit.* Wheaton, Illinois: Victor Books, 1974.

Ford, LeJoy. *Design for Teaching and Training.* Nashville: Broadman Press, 1978.

Friedeman, Matt. *The Master Plan of Teaching.* Wheaton, Illinois: Victor Books, 1990.

Gangel, Kenneth O. *Feeding and Leading.* Wheaton, Illinois: Victor Books, 1989.

Gangel, Kenneth O. *24 Ways to Improve Your Teaching.* Wheaton, Illinois: Victor Books, 1974.

Gangel, Kenneth O. *Unwrap Your Spiritual Gifts.* Wheaton, Illinois: Victor Books, 1984.

Garlett, Marti Watson, *Who Will Be My Teacher?* Waco: Texas: Word Books, 1985.

Grant, Reg and John Reed. *Telling Stories to Touch the Heart.* Wheaton, Illinois: Victor Books, 1990.

Gregory, John Milton. *The Seven Laws of Teaching.* Grand Rapids, Michigan: Baker Book House, 1981.

Haystead, Wes. *Everything You Want to Know about Teaching Young Children.* Ventura, California: Regal Books, 1989.

Haystead, Wes. *Teaching Your Child about God.* Ventura, California: Regal Books, 1981.

Hendricks, Dr. Howard. *Teaching to Change Lives.* Portland, Oregon: Multnomah Press, 1987.

Highet, Gilbert. *The Art of Teaching.* New York: Alfred A. Knopf, 1968.

Horne, Herman H. *The Teaching Techniques of Jesus.* Grand Rapids, Michigan: Kregel, 1974.

Kjos, Berit. *Your Child and the New Age.* Wheaton, Illinois: Victor Books, 1990.

Kuhlman, Edward. *The Master Teacher.* Old Tappan, New Jersey: Fleming H. Revell Co., 1987.

LeBar, Lois. *Education That Is Christian.* Old Tappan, New Jersey: Fleming H. Revell, 1958.

LeBar, Mary. *Children Can Worship.* Wheaton, Illinois: Victor Books, 1976.

LeFever, Marlene D. *Creative Teaching Methods.* Elgin, Illinois: David C. Cook, 1985.

Littauer, Florence. *Raising the Curtain on Children.* Waco, Texas: Word, 1988.

Lopez, Diane D. *Teaching Children: A Curriculum Guide to*

What Children Need to Know at Each Level through Grade Six. Westchester, Illinois: Crossway Books.

Lowrie, Roy. *The Teacher's Heart.* Whittier, California: The Association of Christian Schools International, 1984.

Macaulay, Susan Schaeffer. *For the Children's Sake.* Westchester, Illinois: Crossway Books, 1984.

Packer, James I. *Keeping in Step with Spirit.* Old Tappan, New Jersey: Fleming H. Revell Co., 1984.

Peters, Thomas J. and Robert H. Waterman, Jr. *In Search of Excellence.* New York: Harper and Row, 1982.

Plueddemann, James, Ph.D. *Education That Is Christian.* Wheaton, Illinois: Victor Books, 1989.

Richards, Lawrence O. *Children's Ministry.* Grand Rapids, Michigan: Zondervan Publishing House, 1983.

Shafer, Carl. *Excellence in Teaching with the Seven Laws.* Grand Rapids, Michigan: Baker Book House, 1985.

Schimmels, Cliff. *I Learned It First in Sunday School,* Wheaton, Illinois: Victor Books, 1991.

Selig, George, and Alan Arroyo. *Loving Our Differences.* Virginia Beach, Virginia: CBN Publishing, 1989.

Temple, Joe. *Know Your Child.* Grand Rapids, Michigan: Baker Book House, 1974.

Towns, Elmer. *One Hundred and Fifty-four Steps to Revitalize Your Sunday School.* Wheaton, Illinois: Victor Books, 1989.

Towns, Elmer, *Ten of Today's Most Innovative Churches.* Ventura, California: Regal Books, 1990.

Wagner, C. Peter, *Your Spiritual Gifts Can Help Your Church to Grow.* Ventura, California: Regal Books, 1974.

Williams, Linda VerLee. *Teaching for the Two-Sided Mind.* New York: Simon and Schuster, Inc., 1983.

Willis, Wesley R. *Developing the Teacher in You.* Wheaton, Illinois: Victor Books, 1990.

Willis, Wesley R. *Make Your Teaching Count.* Wheaton, Illinois: Victor Books, 1985.

Wlodkowski, R.J. and J.H. Jaynes. *Eager to Learn: Helping Children Become Motivated and Love Learning.* San Francisco, California: Jossey-Bass Publishers, 1990.

Zuck, Roy B. *The Holy Spirit in Your Teaching.* Wheaton, Illinois: Victor Books, 1984.

Centers

Adventures in Creative Teaching. Wheaton, Illinois: Victor Books, 1986.

Bible Lessons with Learning Centers. Cincinnati, Ohio: Standard Publishing.

Bolton, Barbara J. *How to Do Bible Learning Activities, Grades 1-6,* Ventura, California: Gospel Light Publications, 1982.

Crisci, Elizabeth W. *What Do You Do with Joe? Problem Pupils and Tactful Teachers.* Cincinnati, Ohio: Standard Publications, 1981.

Everybody Ought to Go to Learning Centers. Grand Rapids, Michigan: Baker Book House.

Grogg, Evelyn Leavitt. *Bible Lessons for Little People.* Cincinnati, Ohio: Standard Publications, 1980.

Klein, Karen. *How to Do Bible Learning Activities, Ages 2-5.* Ventura, California: Gospel Light Publications, 1982.

Lee, Rachel Gillespie. *Learning Centers for Better Christian Education.* Valley Forge, Pennsylvania: Judson Press, 1981.

Pratt, David. *Curriculum Design and Development.* New York: Harcourt Brace Jovanovich, Inc., 1980.

Price, Max. *Understanding Today's Children.* Nashville: Convention Press, 1982.

Shining Star Publications
Box 299
Carthage, Illinois 62321

Warren, Ramona. *Preschoolers Can Do Centers,* Elgin, Illinois: David C. Cook, 1991.

Child Development

Ames, Louise Bates, Ph.D., Sidney Baker, M.D., and Frances L. Ilg, M.D. *Child Behavior.* New York: Barnes and Noble Books, a division of Harper and Row Publishers, 1981.

Ames, et al. *Don't Push Your Preschooler,* rev. ed. New York: Harper and Row, 1981.

Ames, *Is Your Child in the Wrong Grade?* Lumberville, Pennsylvania: Modern Learning Press, 1978.

Ames, et al. *Stop School Failure.*

Barbour, Mary A. *You Can Teach 2s and 3s.* Wheaton, Illinois: Victor Books, 1989.

Gangel, Elizabeth and Elsiebeth McDaniel. *You Can Reach Families through Babies.* Wheaton, Illinois: Victor Books, 1986.

Gesell, Arnold, M.D., et al. *The Child from Five to Ten,* rev. ed. New York: Harper and Row, 1977.

Gillis, Don, Marcia and Patty Crawley. *Effective Lesson Planning.* Fort Worth, Texas 76180: Resources for Ministry, 1990.

Ilg, Frances L., M.D. et al. *School Readiness: Behavior Tests Used at the Gesell Institute,* New York: Harper and Row Publishers, 1978.

LeBar, Mary E. and Betty A. Riley. *You Can Teach 4s & 5s.* Wheaton, Illinois: Victor Books, 1987.

McDaniel, Elsiebeth, *You Can Teach Primaries.* Wheaton, Illinois: Victor Books, 1987.

Curriculum

Acorn Children's Publications
Lynchburg, VA 24514

Creative Children's Ministries
7427 Orangethorpe
Suite I
Buena Park, CA 90621

David C. Cook
850 North Grove Avenue
Elgin, IL 60120

Gospel Light
2300 Knoll Drive
Ventura, CA 93003

Group Publishing Co.,
2890 N. Monroe Avenue
Loveland, CO 80538

LifeWay Bible Curriculum
1825 College Avenue
Wheaton, IL 60187

Little People's Pulpit Program
The Train Depot
5015 Tampa West Boulevard
Tampa, FL 33014

One Way Street, Inc.
PUPPETS
Box 2398
Littleton, CO 80161

Scripture Press Publications, Inc.
1825 College Avenue
Wheaton, IL 60187

Standard Publishing
8121 Hamilton Avenue
Cincinnati, OH 45231

Shining Star
Box 299
Carthage, IL 62321

Word and Spirit
6633 Victoria Avenue
Ft. Worth, Texas 76181

Learning Styles
Bates, Marilyn and David Kerisey. *Please Understand Me.* Box
2748, Del Mar, California 92014: Prometheus Nemesis
Book Company.

Carbo, Marie, Rita Dunn, Ed.D., and Kenneth Dunn. *Teaching Students to Read through Their Individual Learning Styles*. Englewood Cliffs, New Jersey: Prentice-Hall, Inc.

Dunn, Kenneth and Rita, Ed.D., *Practical Approaches to Individualizing Instruction*. West Nyack, New York: Parker Publishing Co., Inc., 1972.

Dunn. *Teaching Students through Their Individual Learning Styles*. 11480 Sunset Hills Road, Reston, Virginia 22090: Reston Publishing Co., Inc. (703) 437-8900

Dunn, Rita and Shirley Griggs. *Learning Styles: Quiet Revolution in American Secondary Schools*. National Association of Secondary School Principals. 1904 Associates Drive, Reston, Virginia, 1988.

Gilbert, Anne Green. *Teaching the Three Rs through Movement Experiences*. New York: Macmillan Publishing Co., 1977.

Kolb, David A. *Experiential Learning*. Englewood Cliffs, New Jersey 07632: Prentice-Hall, Inc.

Lawrence, Gordon. *People Types and Tiger Stripes*. Center for Applications of Psychological Type, Inc. P.O. Box 13807, Gainesville, Florida 32604.

Zacharias, Raye. *Styles and Profiles*. 1215 Whispering Lane, Southlake, Texas 76092. (817) 481-4949

Dr. Marie Carbo
Reading Style Inventory
National Reading Styles Institute
Box 39
Roslyn Heights, NE 11577
(800) 331-3117

Kaye Johns and Carol Marshall
Center for Slower Learners
4949 Westgrove, #180
Dallas, TX 75248
(214) 407-9277

Learning Styles Network & Resources
Professor Rita Dunn

Center for Study of Learning and Teaching Styles
St. John's University
Grand Central and Utopia Parkways
Jamaica, NY 11439

The 4MAT System
Bernice McCarthy
EXCEL, Inc.
200 West Station Street
Barrington, IL 60010
(708) 382-7272

Music
Donut Man
Rob Evans
247 Bay Shore
Hendersonville, TN 37015

G.T. Halo Express
(Bible Verses to Music)
1987 King Communications
P.O. Box 24472
Minneapolis, MN 55424

Kids for Kids
Barry McGuire
5490 E. Butler Avenue
Fresno, CA 93727

Integrity Music
1000 Cody Road
Mobile, AL 36695

Maranatha
P.O. Box 1396
Costa Mesa, CA 92626

Motions 'n Music
Scripture Press Publications, Inc.
1825 College Avenue
Wheaton, IL 60187

Mary Rice Hopkins
P.O. Box 362
Montrose, CA 91021

Psalty Tapes
Word, Inc.
5221 N. O'Conner Blvd. Suite 1000
Irving, TX 75039

Salvation Songs for Children
Child Evangelism Fellowship
Warrenton, MO 63383

Sing a Song of Scripture
Lillenas Publications
Kansas City, MO 64141

Spectra
468 McNally Drive
Nashville, TN 37211
Superkids Series

Prayer

Avila, St. Theresa. *A Life of Prayer.* Portland, Oregon: Multnomah Press, 1972.

Bounds, E.M. *Power Through Prayer.* Grand Rapids, Michigan: Baker Book House, 1972.

Christenson, Evelyn. *Lord, Change Me.* Wheaton, Illinois: Victor Books, 1979.

Christenson, Evelyn. *What Happens When Women Pray.* Wheaton, Illinois: Victor Books, 1975.

Foster, Richard J. *Celebration of Discipline.* New York: Harper and Row, 1978.

Getz, Gene A. *Praying for One Another.* Wheaton, Illinois: Victor Books, 1989.

Gofforth, Rosalind. *How I Know God Answers Prayers.* Chicago: Back to the Bible Publishers, Moody Press, 1983.

Marshall, Catherine. *Adventures in Prayer.* Old Tappan, New Jersey: Spire Books, 1975.

Mitchell, Curtis C. *Praying Jesus' Way.* Old Tappan, New Jersey: Fleming H. Revell, 1946.

Murray, Andrew. *With Christ in the School of Prayer.* Westwood, New Jersey: Fleming H. Revell, 1972.

Torrey, R.A. *How to Pray.* Chicago: Moody Press.

Reference Books

Alexander, David and Pat, editors. *Eerdman's Handbook to the Bible.* Grand Rapids, Michigan: William B. Eerdmans Publishing Co., 1973.

Beers, V. Gilbert. *The Victor Handbook of Bible Knowledge.* Wheaton, Illinois: Victor Books, 1981.

Gangel, Kenneth O., Howard G. Hendricks and the Dallas Theological Seminary Christian Education Faculty. *The Christian Educator's Handbook on Teaching.* Wheaton, Illinois: Victor Books, 1980.

Richards, Lawrence O. *The Teacher's Commentary.* Wheaton, Illinois: Victor Books, 1987.

Walvoord, John F. and Roy B. Zuck. *The Bible Knowledge Commentary.* Wheaton, Illinois: Victor Books, 1985.

Wright, Fred. H. *Manners and Customs of Bible Lands.* Chicago: Moody Press, 1953.

Sources for "Doers"

Bolinsky, Mike. *Affirmative Guide to Creative Bible Teaching.* P.O. Box 833, Cedar Hills, Texas 75104. (Many excellent "hands-on" Bible teaching materials for children, youth, and adults, including a twenty-foot whale in which you can conduct a class.)

Cavalletti, Sofia. *The Religious Potential of the Child.* Ramsey, New Jersey 07446: Paulist Press, 1979.

Gettman, David. *Basic Montessori Learning Activities for Under Fives.* New York: St. Martin's Press, 1987.

Montessori, Dr. Maria. *The Absorbent Mind.* One Dag Hammarskjold Plaza, New York, New York 10017: Delta Books, Dell Publishing Co., 1980.

Montessori. *Childhood Education.* New York: A Meridian Book, 1955.

Montessori. *The Montessori Method.* New York: Schocken Books, 1964.

Bible in Living Sound
P.O. Box 234
Norland, WA 98358

Carraway Street, Inc.
Mr. Ron Solomon
200 Frontier City
Chanhassen, MN 55317
(800) 767-0568

CEF Press
P.O. Box 348
Warrenton, Missouri 63383

Christian Educators' Association International
P.O. Box 50025
Pasadena, CA 9115-0025
(818) 795-1983

Comics in the Classroom: A Learning Styles Approach
Canadian Daily Newspaper Publishers Association
890 Yonge Street, #1100
Toronto, Ontario M4W EP4

Cornerstone Curriculum Project
2006 Flatcreek
Richardson, TX 75080
(214) 235-5149

Creative Children's Ministries
7427 Orangethorpe Suite I
Buena Park, CA 90621

Creative Publications
5005 West 110th Street
Oak Lawn, IL 60438

Creative Teachers Publications—Task Cards for Reading
P.O. Box 41
Williston Park, NY 11596

KONOS Character Curriculum
P.O. Box 1534

Richardson, TX 75083
(214) 669-8337

Learning Research Associates, Inc.
P.O. Box 349, Dept. 6
Roslyn Heights, NY 11596

Little Christian Supply
P.O. Box 1763
Blytheville, AR 72316-1763
(for ages 1-3)

Lukens, Betty
Felt Books & Products
P.O. Box 1007
Rohnert Park, CA 94928
(707) 965-3000

National Reading Styles Institute
P.O. Box 39
Roslyn Heights, NY 11577

Marcy Cook Math Materials
P.O. Box 5840
Balboa Island, CA 92662

Mortensen Math
P.O. Box 763068
Dallas, TX 75376
(214) 957-8638

One Way Street, Inc.
P.O. Box 2398
Littleton, CO 80101
(303) 790-1188

The Perfection Form Company
—Reading beyond the Basil (Primary Grades)
—Portals to Reading (Intermediate Grades)
1000 North Second Avenue
Logan, IA 51546

Play 'N Talk
7105 Manzanita Street
Carlsbad, CA 92009
(619) 438-4330

Sing Spell Read & Write
CBN Center
Virginia Beach, VA 23463
(800) 288-4769

Sound Reading Associates
Sharon Briggs & Ginny Sorrell
13704 Springstone Court
Clifton, VA 22024
(703) 266-1044

Sponge Activities
Idea Factory
275 East Pleasant Valley Road
Camarillo, CA 93010

Writing to Think and Thinking to Write
85 Main Street
Watertown, MA 02172

Special Needs
Dennis and Linda Dordigan
3102 Lois Lane
Rowlett, TX 75088
(214) 412-0880
(Available for speaking and music, author of many books,
poems, analogies, and songs)

Joni and Friends
P.O. Box 3333
Agoura Hills, CA 91301

Teacher Training
Celebrate Kids
Dr. Kathryn Kock
P.O. Box 136234
Fort Worth, TX 76136

Child Evangelism Fellowship
2300 E. Highway M
Warrenton, MO 63383-3420

CCMA: Children's Christian Ministries Association
Iris Mears

11314 Woodley Avenue
Granada Hills, CA 91344

Center for Success in Learning
4949 Westgrove #180
Dallas, TX 75248

Resources for Ministries
Teacher Training Videos
Don and Marcia Gillis
6633 Victoria Avenue
Fort Worth, TX 76181

Something Special for Kids
Sam and Sandy Sprott
477 Corona Avenue
Corona, CA 91719